Life in a Crowded Place

Life in a Crowded Place

Making a Learning Community

Ralph Peterson

HEINEMANN
Portsmouth, NH

HEINEMANN
A Division of Reed Publishing (USA) Inc.
361 Hanover Street, Portsmouth, NH 03801-3912
Offices and agents throughout the world

Library of Congress Cataloging-in-Publication Data
Peterson, Ralph, 1933–
    Life in a crowded place : making a learning community / Ralph
Peterson.
      p.   cm.
    Includes bibliographical references.
    ISBN 0-435-08736-3
    1. Group work in education. 2. Classroom environment—United
States. 3. Teaching. I. Title.
LB1032.P48 1992   92-16468
371.3'95—dc20   CIP

Cover design by Maria Szmauz.

Published in the United States of America.
93 94 95 96   9 8 7 6 5 4 3 2

For
Georgia and Ray
Makers of houses, homes,
and communities

Contents

Preface		ix
Acknowledgments		xi
Introduction		1
Part I	**Making a Caring Place**	11
Chapter 1	Ceremony, Ritual, and Rite	15
Chapter 2	Celebration	39
Chapter 3	Conversation	47
Chapter 4	Play	55
Chapter 5	Routines and Jobs	61
Chapter 6	Residency	65
Part II	**Making Sense of Experience**	71
Chapter 7	Putting Language to Work	75
Chapter 8	Parading: Leading and Following	85
Chapter 9	Critique: Discriminating Among Values	91
Chapter 10	Dialogue: Uniting Critique and Inquiry	103
Part III	**Making Learning Communities**	115
Chapter 11	Authority: Empowering Students	119
Chapter 12	Life Activities	127
	Conclusion	137
	Bibliography	141

Preface

This book is intended for teachers who are always reaching for possibility. Teachers who do not stand apart but step wholeheartedly into life with their students and let the dynamics of learning possess them. It takes courage, as well as intelligence and heart, to seek out and create an order that might realize unforeseen potential. These are the people who know the importance of community to life and learning in a crowded place.

Acknowledgments

It is impossible to credit all of the people who have in one way or another contributed to this book. The list is too long. But some people stand out immediately for reading early drafts, contributing insights, ideas, examples, and encouragement. My thanks to Karen Smith, Mary Glover, Linda Sheppard, Margaret Phinney, Maryann Eeds, Kathy Egawa, Audree Miller, Dorothy Watson, Kathy O'Neill Shores, Diana Doyle, Bev Wilcox, Tom Tracy, Barbara Johnston, Maureen Carpenter, Judy Sadowsky, Miriam Merecek, Julia Fournier, Sarah Hudelson, Merri Schall, Karen Lashley, Libby Gilmore, Chris Blessing, Rich Thompson, Ginny Parenza, Lisa Bickley, Kay Vandergrift, Pam Clark, Mike Hagan, Karen Dalrymple, Dwight Vander Schoor, and Krista Sekeres.

Nor can I fail to express my thanks to Dawne Boyer for her insight and the care she took with the manuscript.

Finally, my thanks to Leland B. Jacobs, my teacher, who listened and dialogued with me about these ideas years and years ago.

Introduction

*L*ife in classrooms is an intense social experience. For six hours a day, week after week, month after month, one teacher and anywhere from twenty-two to thirty-four students (sometimes more) live together in a space the size of a large living room. The older the students, the larger the furniture, the tighter the space. At best, it is elbow-to-elbow living. Sometimes learning about reading, social studies, and math is pushed to the side because the complex problems of living together cannot be worked out.

Over the generations, most teachers have managed to cope with the crowded conditions by restricting everything we could think of. Movement. Talk. Note passing. Even handwriting style. You name it, we restricted it. And if the kids were "good," we'd reward them by letting them talk—a little. Even those of us not truly interested in dominating over students posted rules that placed control in our hands. Maintaining control is what we were taught in education courses. Most of us recall our education instructors' warnings on the order of "Don't smile until Thanksgiving" to ensure that students saw only that side of our personality that demanded obedience. And all but a few school administrators take silence as a sign that productive activity is taking place. Manuals and procedures made things easy for us by telling us how to structure our time and how to manage our students' learning. Textbooks and workbooks, designed to keep purposeful order, filled students' desks. And what *really* happened? Students spent their valuable time doing brain-numbing exercises and obeying directions. Instruction of this type has not helped people to think in complicated and critical ways.

Fortunately there have always been teachers who have not only wanted more for their students than participating in a good behavior game and getting the "right" answer to someone else's questions, but have also known how to get the job done. These teachers stand out in my memory (and I am sure they do in yours). They have done more than trust students, call on students to take the initiative, and value what students thought—they had the talent to bring a group together, keep it together, and teach it how to learn together. Their teaching demonstrated that they knew the contribution social life can make to learning. I think of these teachers as being masterful at making learning communities.

Today I believe that there are more teachers than ever who know how to bring learning communities into existence. Like me, most of them had to stumble on to it. It happened my second year of teaching when I was assigned to teach a multi-age class of eight to twelve year olds. Textbooks and teaching guides written for specific grade levels were of no use. I had no choice but to rethink what my teaching was about. *Good things did not happen right away.* This, more than anything, is important to remember. We need to know that we are not failures if we do not have overnight successes. Age-old wisdom tells us that things of worth take time to achieve. This is especially true when what we seek requires a change in perception. That year I made the most important discovery I have ever made about teaching: *community in itself is more important to learning than any method or technique.* When community exists, learning is strengthened—everyone is smarter, more ambitious, and productive. Well-formed ideas and intentions amount to little without a community to bring them to life.

That experience, which happened over thirty years ago, continues to guide me. Although the concept of community in the classroom is not new, what is new is insight into why it is so important. We know now that the way human beings learn has nothing to do with being kept quiet. It has to do with our desire to make sense of our experience, to join with others, to become a part of a community. It has to do with developing our expressive abilities and participating in everything that interests us, with being able to benefit from the insight and experience of others as we work at making the world take on meaning for ourselves, with living and learning in a place outfitted with opportunities to learn, a place where we can fumble and make mistakes without being scorned or laughed at. And it has to do with being responsible for our own learning. In short, it has to *mean* something to us. And it won't unless we ourselves make it mean something. We need to learn how to talk about that meaning to truly understand our thinking. We need to listen to how others interpret our meaning in order to deepen our own understanding.

This is what happens in a learning community. Life in a learning community is helped along by the interests, ideas, and support of others. Social life is not snuffed out; it is nurtured and used to advance learning in the best way possible. Caring and interest of others breathes purpose and life into learning. Learning is social. The work of Vygotsky (1978) calls attention to the importance of others where learning is concerned. The position taken is that learning awakens a variety of internal processes that operate only when the child is interacting with others in his environment and in cooperation with his peers. Even mainstream educators are beginning to recognize that education fails when it focuses solely on the accumulation of demonstrable facts and skill. An image is taking shape that acknowledges a more complex and irreducible phenomenon, the social person.

One could use the word "family" to describe life in a learning community, since the same underlying structures that appear in a healthy family occur in the classroom. Not many parents keep their children still and quiet all day long. They encourage their children to be expressive, to collaborate, to take risks, and to learn from failure by reflecting on what has happened. Isn't it only common sense for teachers to put the same principles to use in school? As teachers, we can choose to provide a healthy place for our students—a place where they belong and are helped to grow in their learning, feeling, and thinking.

Should you doubt the importance of community to learning, talk to teachers in the middle school and the primary grades who teach multi-age classes. The second year I taught a multi-age class and more than half of the students returned from the previous year's class, I thought I was in heaven. We didn't have to start from zero in making our community. Newcomers were initiated into an existing community. Students knew what to do, and the caring ways that had been established came back into play. Rigorous intellectual activity got underway with surprising ease because we could draw on the studies we had conducted during the previous year. There was a knowledge base to work from that the previous year had taken months to develop. We came together as if we had been apart for a long weekend.

What I will do in this book is name and describe what teachers do in making learning communities and make a connection with how we structure our lives in the family and the neighborhood. The idea behind my work is simple. We who teach need new ways to think about teaching and learning. For decades talk about teaching has centered on the importance of educational objectives, selection of learning experiences, organization of learning experiences, and evaluation. I do not question that this orientation has some value. The problem is that it is terribly one-sided. Teaching is complex work. No one, two, or three ways of viewing can address the complexity. It's my hope that the concept of community uncovers another possibility for understanding the work teachers undertake.

Throughout the book I contrast what we've come to know as traditional teaching and holistic teaching. I'm uneasy about making statements that divide teachers and their practice. I considered myself to be a good teacher even when a part of my work and the students' learning amounted to acting out someone else's plan. Like all teachers, I have taught next door to those who kept to the textbooks and were considered by colleagues, students, and parents to be good teachers. But I think that we need to subject our own assumptions to criticism and stop being afraid to change and grow. It's what we expect of our students; we'd be doing a disservice to them and ourselves not to follow suit.

Traditional teaching usually focuses on demonstrated behavior and mastery of specified knowledge and skills. Knowledge is presented as if it were unchanging and compartmentalized; as if learning can be reduced to completing exercises and activities. It's not important for students to express themselves in original ways, since they don't contribute to their own knowing. A teacher whose philosophical orientation is traditional might stand at the front of the class, confident that he or she has all the knowledge and is responsible for giving that knowledge to the students who sit at their desks with minds like blank slates waiting to be filled.

A traditional teacher might also think of making learning easier by breaking the complex down into the simple. A language arts teacher, for example, might use textbooks that break concepts down into grammatical parts to have students learn the building blocks of language—letters to words, words to sentence, sentences to paragraphs—before teaching them to write ideas. But what really happens? Students drill on fragments of language—they don't construct meaning or think for themselves. How many of us remember diagramming sentences in school? How many of us who consider ourselves to be quite literate can or have any interest in diagramming sentences now? Is it fair to limit students' thinking to these types of exercises?

Unfortunately, strictly traditional teaching has neglected a very important dimension of the way our minds work. People are meaning makers; we seek order and draw on images and feelings as well as thoughts. Our minds are not built to be only logical; intuition and the arts are also ways of knowing.

Learning is aided by experiencing wholes, not just bits and pieces. We need to experience the big picture in order to make sense of all the little details, and this is where holism comes in. In writing about community, I have had the support of a good many teachers who approach their teaching from a "whole language" orientation. These teachers extend their teaching concerns beyond the intellectual. Study and experience has taught them that language and learning are social. Therefore, they work to bring students together and foster caring relationships. They recognize the important roles that literature and the arts can play in the education of the imagination. In this book, however, I do not explicitly refer to whole language teaching and teachers. Although I have chosen to make reference to holism and holistic teaching, I hope that the ideas will be viewed as supportive of the philosophy, practice, and intent of whole language teachers.

Traditional teachers who want to learn about holistic teaching have to change their ways of thinking about learning and a broad range of practices. The answers to their questions are not in a manual. Support groups, where members share their thinking and talk about problems, can help teachers develop their beliefs and practices and encourages them to take risks and strengthen their resolve. Collaboration in the learning community and the faculty room is a strength of teachers who advocate holism. We all need to see that we have different ways of viewing the world, and that differences are important to understand in order to get the whole picture. The following chart illustrates the changes in practice and thought that might occur if a teacher were to shift from a strictly traditional practice toward that of a more holistic perspective. The key word is *toward*. All important is the intent behind the direction teaching takes.

From Traditional Thought & Practices Characterized By:	**Toward Holistic Thought & Practices Characterized By:**
Teacher Orientation To ensure and achieve stated objectives	**Teacher Orientation** To help students grow in complicated and critical ways
View of Knowledge Exists outside the person—person does not contribute to meaning	**View of Knowledge** People construct meaning by bringing meaning to and taking meaning from their experiences
Skill-Based Teaching Skill mastery is of foremost concern	**Meaning-Centered Teaching** Knowledge is personal—people search for meaning, structure, order
Skills Learned in isolation for the purpose of mastery	**Skills** Learned while engaged in authentic expression that requires meaning to be negotiated, expressed, and developed
Curriculum Is standardized; guided by scope and sequence documents and commercial materials	**Curriculum** Is negotiated; connected to students' lives and supports students taking a critical stance
Reductionism Is a principle; learning is best achieved by reducing the complexity of what is to be learned	**Connectedness** Is a principle; what makes sense to the students is built upon in order to further understanding

Correctness
Is valued foremostly

Approximation
Is an accepted principle

Conceptual Knowledge
Is *the* valued way of knowing

Intuition, Feeling, and Conceptual Knowledge
Are valued ways of knowing

Obedience
Is required in a classroom controlled by the teacher

Collaboration
Is essential as teacher and student construct a learning community together

Discipline
Students are controlled through such methods as assertive discipline and token reinforcement

Discipline
Students are empowered and responsible for themselves and to the group

Schooling
Is viewed as preparation for the future

Schooling
Emphasizes the importance of a meaningful present

Needs
Cognitive emphasized

Interests
Social, emotional, and cognitive are important

Work
Focus is on individualization of instruction

Work
Collaboration and negotiation of meaning are emphasized

Accountability
Teacher is held accountable for student's learning

Accountability
Student is held accountable for own learning

Students
Carry out plans made for them

Students
Participate in planning and evaluation

Competence
Judged by test performance

Competence
Judged by demonstrated ability to express meaning, solve problems, work with others, make perceptive critiques

7

Continuity	**Continuity**
Controlled through curriculum	Teacher and students seek out continuity within the life of the group and individual students' lives

Throughout the book, I talk about these differences and illustrate the ways in which teachers go about making learning communities based on the holistic framework.

There are teachers who seem to teach effortlessly from a holistic perspective, but they are not the majority. The plain truth is that for most of us, it's hard work to rework our belief system, and it's equally hard to translate our thinking into action. In holism, there is no destination or schedule. There is only thinking, doing, imagining what might be, and trying again. And let's face it. Breaking with traditions is certain to be an uphill pull. We who teach were once first graders. At age six we were initiated into school life and began sorting out the roles of teacher and student. We were, in the same sense as goslings and ducklings, "imprinted." It is no wonder that teachers have a hard time and that parents and policy makers find it difficult to support change. We belong to schooling traditions more than they belong to us. Even when we become convinced that traditional ways don't always work, change is difficult, in part because traditional practices and materials are supported by policies and procedures that mandate their use. Developers of commercial materials have lobbied to make sure it works that way. Where I live, it's a major victory for teachers to be "allowed" to purchase trade books with money that is budgeted for workbooks. Education is a big-money business, and make no mistake about it—it's a political business, too.

And yet change does occur. If this were not true, students would still be under the rule of the hornbook and hickory stick. The likelihood of change is increased when there is a significant shift in societal needs. Are we at such a point today? The fact that the world around us is changing so rapidly suggests that we are.

In this book, I give ideas about why teachers do what they do when they make learning communities. The book is organized into three parts. Part One focuses on how ritual, rites, ceremony, conversation, celebration, and play function in creating a place, a learning community. Part Two gives attention to teaching about the world by means of "parading," critique, and dialogue. And Part Three talks about language, the issues of authority, and engaging students in real live learning experiences. Holistic teachers conduct their work within a highly complex structure. We need only to take a look through another lens to see it.

1

Making a Caring Place

*T*eachers who make communities have a big order to fill. Students who show up at the classroom door when the school bell rings in the fall are not an all-of-a-kind family. Far from it. Each person is unique, a reflection of his or her own personality. It is not unusual for friends, who take bites from the same sandwich and come from the same neighborhood, to come away from an experience with different observations, feelings, and interpretations of what has happened. What is more, it is not unusual in today's classrooms to find three, five, and sometimes more cultures represented. Bringing students together as a group and nurturing tolerance for their ways and beliefs while celebrating their differences challenges the talents of the most experienced teachers.

Teachers who make communities with their students are cultural engineers of sorts. The primary goal at the beginning of a new year or term is to lead students to come together, form a group, and be there for one another. At first students are concerned foremost with their own welfare. It is by establishing values of caring and trust in the classroom that social ties and interest in one another's welfare comes into existence. Making meaning requires students to be responsible for their own learning, collaborate with others, and learn from their failures as well as their successes. Students don't need to be in agreement with one another, but they do need to see themselves as being responsible for others and find value in group life. The teacher takes the lead in making him or herself into a trusted person. How can it be done?

If learning community is important, it would be a big help to identify the underlying structures that teachers and students use, often unconsciously, to make it all work. (I think of a learning community as something that teachers and students actively construct together.) Elements names the building blocks teachers and students use in making learning communities. Just as painters work with the elements of point, line, tone, and plane, teachers and students use ceremony, ritual, rite, celebration, play, and critique when they make a learning community. These elements are as old as humankind. When students do routines and chores, celebrate, converse with one another, engage in rituals and ceremonies, and give and receive criticism, they are doing what is an everyday part of their lives. The living and learning that occurs in the classroom is shaped by the same cultural forms humankind has developed over the ages.

Holistic teaching-learning draws on traditional cultural forms to create an orderly place for learning. Contrary to popular belief, holistic learning communities are highly structured places. In the chapters that follow, we'll take a look at how traditional cultural forms—elements—are used to make these orderly places, as well as how they work.

1

Ceremony, Ritual, and Rite

School is a temporary place that is open for six hours a day for about nine months. It is not the dominant reality in students' lives. There are students who skip school to participate in other activities, and at age sixteen some students choose to drop out. Teachers face the challenge of creating a place where students feel they belong and where they want to be. In making learning communities with their students, teachers make use of ceremony, ritual, and rite in an effort to create a place where students feel they belong.

In our daily lives, we use the words "ceremony," "ritual," and "rite" without making distinctions. We talk about a marriage ceremony, a marriage ritual, and a marriage rite, and we have the same idea in mind. Even dictionary definitions of the terms overlap. In this chapter, I want to explore how these terms contribute separately to shaping social life and learning in the classroom.

Ceremony

To appreciate the function of ceremony in the life of the learning community, we must look upon life there as distinct from life at home and in the neighborhood. Learning communities fit what Berger and Luckmann (1967) refer to as "finite provinces of meaning." All finite provinces of meaning are marked by a turning away of attention from the reality of everyday life. Ceremonies aid students in making the transition between daily life and classroom living by turning thoughts toward schooling.

Why is ceremony so important in the holistic learning community, when it has not really been an issue in the traditional classroom? Because textbook programs demand little of students in the way of imagination and initiative, ceremony is of little importance. Obedience and following directions is what counts, as students take away one text and take out the next. But ceremony becomes very important when students are expected to construct meaning on their own and with others. Assuming responsibility for their own learning and not merely acting out someone else's plan calls upon students to focus their attention. Where study is concerned, ceremony brings about an internal readiness, pushing aside that which might interfere and helping students to participate wholeheartedly by concentrating thought and feeling on the work at hand.

Opening the Day

Because events occurring in the learning community are out of the ordinary, opening ceremonies are important. There are few other places in life where a group of peers, except for the leader, gather in a room to work at learning. What is more, the learning is both particular and calculated to take place along more or less predictable lines. Teachers, in seeking to make these out of the ordinary places, these finite provinces of meaning, real to students, employ ceremony.

What happens when no opening ceremony is used? A friend, who taught in Massachusetts at the time the U.S. Supreme Court ruled against

16

reading the Bible as part of the opening ceremony in school, discovered that there was a side to the issue that the Court had not taken into consideration. He knew about the decision but gave no thought to how to get the morning underway, and he found himself in front of the class without a plan for getting the school day started. After a bit of hesitation, he resorted to saying, "Take out your reading book," and the class stumbled into the day. Everyone felt disgruntled. It took more than a week of working with the students to develop an opening ceremony that would bring the day to a proper opening for everyone.

In 1879, John Ogden wrote about the importance of ceremony to life in classrooms:

> Presently a rapid succession of heavy raps, or the loud ringing of the bell, is heard in the vicinity of the teacher's desk; and through all, and above all, the sentorian voice of the teacher is heard calling to order (?). By repeated effort and great exertions, this is so far accomplished at length, that one accustomed to such scenes would hardly be mistaken to the intention, at least. Order being thus far secured, without one moment's reflection, to say nothing about opening exercises of a formal character, the classes are called and the teacher and pupils rush into the arena of duties to contend, to fret and sweat (I will not say swear) over the day's difficulties (13).

Ogden believed that when days have such a beginning, the teacher and the students are not in a proper frame of mind to "encounter the perplexing duties as will most likely meet them" (13). Ogden emphasized the importance of reflection and gaining a readiness for the day's activities. Ceremony creates an intellectual and emotional order for the schooling activity so that the group is focused upon learning and community life.

Properly executed, an opening ceremony will get the group off to a good beginning. Flag salutes and patriotic songs are often incorporated into ceremonies. Too, there are teachers who open with a song and a class meeting to share thoughts and outline a plan for the day. Still other teachers begin with a period of meditation. A friend of mine who teaches junior high school begins each class period with ten minutes of silent writing. Class periods are short and she has found that a brief period of writing gets students to settle down and ready themselves for studying English.

Tom Tracy thinks of his opening ceremony as a version of "show and tell." First thing in the morning, students who want to share sign-up for either "morning announcements" or "acknowledge and appreciate." Time to begin is signaled by a student ringing a bell and the sharing begins with students in charge.

The morning I visited Tom's classroom, he had written on the board:

1. **Good Morning !**
   Be Prepared:
   ▲ Paper and Pencil
   ▲ Literature Book

2. **You need your writers' notebook ready for the first thing we do.**

3. **Getting Ready.**
   During this time, class jobs are done by students: animals are cared for, the library and other areas are made ready for the day. Students sit in groups at tables. Attendance is taken by one member of the group and another student collects the homework and records who has handed it in on a chart.

4. **Morning Announcements**
   Tell about what is coming up in your lives.
   Examples: Planning to go to the library after school, visits to classmates' homes, family trips, and weekend plans.
   Share what is happening in your family life.
   Here students tell about family events, including birthdays, trips, marriages, visitors, pets, and members of their families. If there is anything noteworthy occurring in the neighborhood, it is usually presented here.

5. **Acknowledging and appreciating people at home and in the class.**
   Students acknowledge people who are deserving of recognition and tell why. Tom emphasizes students acknowledging personal achievements.

Tom's opening ceremony not only gets the day started, but it also nurtures values important to community life. Knowing about the other person is the seed that can blossom into authentic caring. In turn, caring strengthens the pulse of community life. The strength of all social relationships and communities arises out of caring. Caring for another person, in the most significant sense, is to help him or her grow and self-actualize (Mayeroff 1971). I see this opening ceremony as a smart way to go about making a community of people who are knowledgeable about one another.

In education, the quality of social life in the classroom and its influence on learning is now receiving unprecedented attention and well it should. It is the greatest good where learning is concerned. Mayeroff treats caring as a process, a way of relating that involves development. The way that teachers choose to begin the school day can contribute to the knowing one another that fosters caring.

Whatever way the teacher chooses to begin the day, the opening ceremony inevitably incorporates ritual such as saluting the flag, singing a good-morning song, listening to a poem, or doing the calendar.

During the Day

Once into the school day, teachers use ceremony to create order in much the same way that chapters bring order to the content of a rich and varied narrative. Ceremony can clear the air of ideas, emotion, and work patterns before taking up a new activity. When ceremony is not used, there is a sense of jumping from one activity to the next without a sense of purpose. Good ceremony provides time and a suitable climate for students to come to grips with the forthcoming activity.

Take as an example students who have been working at literature study and who now are going to shift their attention to mathematics. A song or movement activity, even the entire group stretching, can close the involvement in story and ready students for thinking mathematically. Ceremony that opens a writer's workshop is another example. Gathering students together in a particular area in the room, conducting a ritual mini-lesson that settles students down even if it does not inform, and sharing what work individuals will be undertaking are other examples of ceremony at work.

Ending the Day

When the day has run its course, ceremony can be used to pull elements together, make them whole. Not all teachers close the day with ceremony. In some classrooms, activity collapses when the bell rings. Students shove books and papers into their desks, grab their coats, and line up while the teacher makes announcements.

When teachers use a touch of ceremony to make the day complete, the working rhythms of the day are slowed; loose ends are tied. Students are brought together to end on a harmonious note. Some teachers bring students together and ask them to share something important that has happened during the day. Other teachers recount the day's events with their students, noting achievements, pointing toward tomorrow. Singing together, having the class historian report the day's events, or gathering in groups to converse before leaving are other ways. I heard about a junior high school community that closed its day with a ritual dance movement. Regardless of how ceremony is incorporated, the intent is to establish a feeling of completeness before the students return to the everyday world beyond the classroom walls.

Ceremony aids teachers in bringing shape and life to the learning community. It forms attitudes and creates a feeling of group purpose. It can fire emotions, affect a contemplative mood, and foster or bring about an internal order. We achieve harmony and seriousness with ceremony. It's a powerful tool to help us center the group and turn attention to the events that are to follow.

Ritual

Ritual is a way of connecting to a larger community. It is more than talk. It is made up of symbolic acts that ground family and community life. Rituals such as taking up a position in a circle, taking oaths, making pledges, and lighting candles all symbolize that participants are entering into a different reality.

In elementary school classrooms, ritual is easily sighted when it is time for a story. In Miriam Merecek's class, when it is time for story, the student in charge moves Miriam's comfortable chair to a corner of the room, takes the story candle out of the cupboard, and sets it in the center of a small table. When the candle is lighted, students stop whatever they are doing and gather together to hear the story. The candle lighting signals that a different reality is being summoned, one that requires students to enter into imaginary worlds. In Karen Smith's class, students move to a carpeted area of the room where comfortable pillows are set about. When Karen takes her seat and opens the book, conversations stop and the story commands everyone's attention. When Diana Doyle moves to her rocker with a book in her hand, her stance at the chair and the book signals it is time to gather for a story. Everyone knows what to do at that moment. They stop their work, choose a spot on the floor, and ready themselves to entertain a story.

These rituals help students to leave the here-and-now of community life and give themselves to the imaginary world of story. When the story is over, the teacher will close the book or snuff out the candle, bringing the world of story to a close. Once the ritual is established, all of this is done effortlessly, without directions.

In another class, it's writing time. Students go about getting ready in a variety of ways. Luke gets up and sharpens four or five pencils. Duncan opens his notebook, smooths the pages, cups his chin in his hands, and stares out the window. April organizes her desk before opening her notebook to read over what she's already written. Jayce organizes paper and colored pencils and begins his writing by drawing a picture. With startling consistency, writers act out their way of readying themselves for writing.

It is not surprising to find ritual a part of learning community life. From the time we get up in the morning until we turn out the light before bed, we perform rituals. Ritual is an integral part of all life; it gives expression to meaning, both ordinary and sacred. It exists in weddings and conversations, in giving birth and dying, and in bathing and praying. We all participate in rituals, whether we're making the morning coffee or playing games. The significance of ritual to life is studied from numerous perspectives, including biogenetic, religious, political, and economic.

Susan Langer (1951) sees ritual as symbolically transforming experiences that no other form of expression can adequately express. She writes that human life is shot through with ritual and that "it is an intricate fabric of reason and rite, of knowledge and religion, prose and poetry, fact and dream" (49). Ritual can express feelings, experience, and dispositions when other forms of expression fail us. That is why we behave in certain ways at funerals, gather in specific ways during holidays, and participate in reunions. Through ritual, we express value, being, and commitment.

Ritual appeals to the imagination and the heart. And it is exacting—the "right" way of conducting a ritual has to be learned. (Take note of how, when you are in an unfamiliar situation, you observe others very closely to see the way things are done.) If you doubt that rituals need to be conducted in certain ways, talk to teachers who give ritual treatment of the calendar as part of the opening ceremony. Substitute teachers seldom do it right, and when the "real" teacher returns, students are sure to tell about the sorry way the substitute conducted the opening ceremony.

When ritual is incorporated into an opening ceremony, it gets every-body on the same page, so to speak. Bev Wilcox speaks about getting a "flow of intersubjectivity" among community members. In her opening ceremony, she calls on students and asks how they feel, what they're think-ing, what it is they're looking forward to doing during the day. This is not only an orderly way to begin the day, but it also gives community members personal insight into their schoolmates' feelings and thoughts and rein-forces social ties.

Ritual has a centering effect. Think of the times you have had to forgo the opening ceremony because school started with a special event. Once back in the classroom, it's not smooth sailing. When I participate in ritual, I experience a "standing-in," or "living" of meaning. What I mean by this is that I need not search for the right words to say or worry about what to do next. My body knows what to do. Ritual makes it possible to dwell in an experience, to exist in feeling ways, to simply be one with the moment.

Ritual allows teachers to use one of humankind's most prized forms of expressing meaning and creating order. Students bring the rituals of home and neighborhood with them to school. The rituals of greeting and caring for one another, and those that are a part of work, play, conversation, argument, and friendship, exist naturally and require little effort or notice on the teacher's part. Teachers rely on the effortless contribution ritual makes to an orderly and meaningful place of caring and learning. But ritual can also be used to strengthen community ties—it can play a part in creating a desired mood, bring definition to a place in the room, center students, and release the imagination.

To avoid confusion, ritual as it is discussed here is of a kind not usually associated with schooling. I am not referring to ritual as it exists in reading group circles, which usually does not intensify and enliven the spirit, but, as often as not, numbs the mind and imagination. Ritual can easily become a routine response that deadens involvement. Should that happen, ritual, like the weekly spelling test, becomes an end in itself, and that threatens students' opportunities to learn and enjoy. Deeper level involvement is denied, as teacher and students act out patterned behavior for its own sake.

I find it useful to organize thinking about ritual into two categories: individual (or personal) rituals and community rituals. Individual rituals, as illustrated in the class where students differed in their approaches to writing, need not be shared or practiced by the group to exist. Community rituals, on the other hand, as illustrated by the class that participated in story time in the same manner, are practiced by the group.

Individual Rituals

Individual rituals are the predictable, personal acts we perform in the process of creating an internal order or desired disposition. Just as we act out an individual ritual when we rise in the morning and prepare for the day (talk to people about the individual ways they "have to" brush their teeth, and you'll understand how important these rituals are), a student will perform a ritual when settling into a good book. The right chair has to be sat in, the right position assumed, the book held in such a way. This ritual can be as important to literary experience as getting up on the right side of the bed is to getting the day off to a good start.

Students (and all of us) adopt ritual without even knowing it. For most, a pattern of behavior simply evolves. But teachers can help by pointing out a series of actions that might center students in their work. Some students might clear their work space except for the bare necessities. Others might scoot off to a spot with a friend and settle in together. Of course, it takes time for individual rituals to evolve fully: after all, they are personal. To alert yourself to ritual of writing, you might take note of what it is you go through in getting ready to write. One friend of mine writes in a bathrobe and never takes a shower before writing. Another never settles down to write until the house has been put into good order. Give thought to what it is that you write with and what kind of paper it is that you write on. The place where a person writes is another factor. Some require a comfortable chair. I am always surprised at the number of people who do their writing on their bed. Others write at the kitchen table where the refrigerator is close at hand. Food and drink are a part of some writers' rituals. We have our way of settling into our writing.

Students who "stick to the edge," unable or unwilling to accept responsibility and give their all to the work at hand, can be upsetting to most teachers. Students who have exact rituals for setting their feet in the batter's box and readying themselves for the pitch, can be lost when it comes to getting to work with books and expressing themselves on paper. When this happens, I see if a personal ritual will help them settle into their work. I join them in studying how others go through ritual acts and help them develop their own to try out. I have always found it more useful to work in this way than to worry about what it is they don't know. The point is that students must get started at their work on their own. Once underway, the work will inform the teacher about what might be done to bring about further development. Students can be put into their seats and forced to do fake work, but that will never lead to genuine growth.

Community Rituals

This type of ritual can best be observed in activities such as celebration, play, conversation, and dialogue. Although the experience of community ritual is internal, the symbolic transformation of experience is open to view. Community rituals differ in kind. Rituals of the home and community are choreographed behavior. Play the national anthem and we stand up automatically. We greet one another in predictable ways, join in conversations in ways others understand, and line up for movie tickets or to get a drink without giving it a thought. Game rituals of the school yard are passed down as younger players work their way into playing, just as rituals that bring order to the school dance are passed down.

Community rituals are best when they're rooted in students' lives and when they develop as community members work at living and working together. Reason does not guide their development so much as feeling does. What is more, where ritual is concerned there is a "right" way to conduct oneself. If you doubt this, attend a junior high school dance and observe how the boys and girls greet one another, how they stand, and how they come together to dance. One teacher in Oregon told me that after lunch each day she gathered her students around to read to them.

One day as she read, a student began to massage her shoulders. A week later, a ritual had evolved. Once the story was completed, students stayed on the rug, scooted into a circle, massaged the shoulders of the students in front of them, and shared their ideas about the story. One day a child commented, "This is the very nicest part of our day." Genuine participation in a ritual act amounts to more than being a member of the group; it signals agreement with the values, disposition, rules, and beliefs that are shared by the members.

We who teach might turn to ritual when we want students to enter into an activity in a particular frame of mind. Through symbols and symbolic acts, we clear the way for contemplation, entertaining fanciful images and deepening our understanding of what we discuss. When students perform rituals such as moving to another place in the classroom and gathering in a circle for story time, what happens can be likened to the lowering of the house lights and raising of the curtain at a play: the audience is moved to give themselves to the imaginary world created through words. When the play is over, when the enjoying and dialogue has come to an end, the audience leaves in as orderly a way as they entered.

Ritual is not restricted to literary and other aesthetic activities. When a group has to attend to a particular event, ritual is often a part of ceremony, functioning to draw the group together and focus its attention. Just as saluting the flag and listening to principal's announcements get the program off to an orderly beginning in school assemblies, rituals are important when members of a class make presentations about science projects. There is a way of acting that is predictable. The student and the topic are introduced. Someone asks the student how he or she became interested in the topic and finally assures the student that the group is looking forward to the presentation. These preliminaries settle people in and ready both the presenter and the audience for what is to follow.

Celebrating students' achievements can be a powerful force on the side of learning, whether students are young or old. And it is to ritual we turn to intensify the spirit. Although people are experienced in performing rituals, it can be a challenge to develop the right ritual for a given occasion. I find that it helps to think about birthday celebrations, events everyone enjoys and participates in, to get me thinking about how ritual might be used. Birthday celebrations demonstrate how ritual symbols and actions, including eating and granting of privilege, contribute to the spirit of the celebration. Birthday celebrations centered on ritual acts of giving cards and singing songs strengthen the community by symbolically affirming the importance of each student's life.

Of course, it takes more than a rug, a patterned movement, a lighted candle, a special chair (such as an author's chair), a song, or a chant to use the power of ritual in making a learning community. To be a symbolic force, the people participating have to accept ritual as a valued way of experiencing. Students must be willing to leave the world of their daily concerns behind and to participate with sincerity. Ritual involves a willingness to give of oneself in feeling ways and cannot be forced. The song has but one way to be sung and the chant is chanted in union with others. A sense of oneness rises out of the shared communal acts when properly performed, thereby instilling the symbolic act with power.

Limitations of Ritual

The value of ritual rests in symbolic expression; therefore, the meaning experienced by participating in ritual cannot be spelled out. But that does not mean the act is not significant. In celebrating your friends' anniversary, imagine bypassing the ritual toasts, tributes, and gifts. Who among us would go to the work and expense of a Thanksgiving celebration, if a comparable experience could be had by reading a paragraph from a book on Thanksgiving? The ritual treatment of food, song, and telling of stories enables us to dwell within an event of our own making that frees us to search out unity between the past and the present.

Ritual is a double-edged sword. Life controlled through ritual moves smoothly and with little effort. Re-visit a familiar event. The circle is formed, words and story are introduced, reading responsibility is passed from one student to the next, and questions are asked. The group is dismissed to take up workbooks, and a new group of students takes up the circled chairs. Students know their parts and respond on cue. Neither teacher nor students are open to emergent possibilities or strive to exercise their critical abilities; the object is to complete the ritual with as few hitches as possible. (More than one teacher conducting a reading group—sitting on a small chair—has begun to doze, lost balance, tipped the chair over, and found herself on the floor!) This is a misuse of ritual, since it is extended into the learning act itself by conditioning students to respond to a set of circumstances in a mindless way, rather than positioning them to see and think for themselves. Ritual properly used does not result in deadening initiative. At best, ritual functions to keep students in touch with themselves, forge community bonds, and liberate imagination.

Rite

At first, I didn't see rite as an important part of life in the learning community—I thought the orientation might be too formal. Still, I couldn't drop the idea, so I began to pay attention and listen more carefully to my teaching partners. In time, I discovered that teachers do mark times of passage by actions that qualify as rites. I turned to a work by Van Gennep, first published in 1908 and reprinted in 1960, to find a structure for thinking about rites in the learning community. There I found exciting ideas that were helpful in leading me to better understand the significance of rites in teaching. What I have to say about rite doesn't stand apart on its own. Rite, like ritual, finds its expression within other elements like ceremony and celebration (discussed in the next chapter).

Before identifying the kinds of rites I see function in learning communities, here is Van Gennup (1960) on rites:

> The life of an individual in any society is a series of passages from one age to another. Whenever there are fine distinctions among age or occupational groups, progression from one group to the next is accompanied by special acts . . . so that [a person's] life comes to be made up of a succession of stages with similar ends and beginnings: birth, social, puberty, marriage, [parenthood], advancement to a higher class, occupational specialization, and death. For every one of these events there are ceremonies whose essential purpose is to enable the individual to pass from one defined position to another which is equally well defined (2–3).

I see three kinds of rite occurring in learning communities: *transition*, *incorporation*, and *separation*. In daily living, we don't consciously engage in rites. They happen. It's possible to stand apart from ritual acts, analyze what is happening, and speculate on the significance of the acts. But when you are one of the people participating in a rite, you are simply doing what any person would do in that same situation. The great advantage in naming rites as far as teaching and learning are concerned is that we can exercise greater control in establishing what is of value in the learning community.

Transition Rite

This category can be further divided into two aspects of how teachers work to bring order to learning communities: *threshold rites* and *competency rites.*

Threshold rites. Human beings have forever used defined boundaries to set places apart. Members of an Athabascan community I lived in on the Yukon River in the early 1960s hunted and fished in defined territories that were passed on traditionally through the family. One family traveled sixty miles below the village to hunt. Towns, cities, states, regions, and nations are all defined by boundaries. When we cross national boundaries, we undergo certain rites. Our passports and papers are reviewed, our luggage is checked, and our passports stamped. Territories exist in cities. Some territories have a gate, making entrance possible only with the appropriate windshield sticker and personal identification. Other territories are not so clearly marked, but they nonetheless exist. We have descriptions such as East Side, West Side, uptown, and downtown to describe some of them. Small towns are to outsiders territories in themselves, but to the people in them there are major divisions.

The threshold marks the territory of the learning community. Entering and leaving the classroom, crossing the threshold into a finite province of meaning to ensure that learning happens, and then leaving the learning community to return to everyday life of home and neighborhood are important transitions. In my experience, we who teach differ greatly not only in how we handle the transition but in the results realized.

Think of a time your students entered the classroom in an unacceptable way only to be "marched" right back over the threshold to the playground. Once lectured to (with the closing words, "Now, let's see if we can get it right"), students return to cross the threshold again in an acceptable manner. Crossing the threshold in the "right" way acknowledges that students are aware that they are making a passage from one world, so to speak, to another. Young students know the importance of thresholds.

As they grow up, they're denied entrance (especially when it comes to older brothers' and sisters' rooms!) into certain places in their own homes.

What thresholds we choose to cross and how we cross them says a good deal about who we are and what we value. Think of the thresholds you will not cross because the meaning contained on the other side is not acceptable to you. In the small town where I grew up, women didn't go into the bar except on a celebration day. Too, the manner in which we cross thresholds is determined by the meaning existing on the other side. A funeral requires ushers to help people across the threshold. At a concert, people are slowed at the entrance just long enough to have their tickets taken. When the the sign "TESTING" is on a classroom door, we cross the threshold quietly.

There are many different kinds of thresholds and many different ways of crossing. Guests wait at the threshold to be welcomed into our home, but friends cross after giving the door a knock. People who value privacy cross thresholds that signal others not to follow, and antagonists draw a line between themselves and dare each other to cross. Rites carried out at the threshold are transition rites when the crossing brings the person into meaning of a different order.

In the early days of the school year, students can be hesitant about crossing this important threshold; the finite province of meaning on the other side can raise uncertainty. Teachers give great care to helping young children cross the threshold. In kindergarten, teachers often invite parents to come with their children on the opening days of school and stick around until the child settles in and moves about confidently. It's just as important that older students are helped to make the transition. Feeling comfortable and confident in a situation is a necessary condition for people to give their best. At times, we fail to recognize how unique the meaning, rules, and expectations contained in the classroom are. To ensure that high school and college students get introduced to the diversity of campus life in a positive way, programs are set up to inform students about what will be expected of them in different situations. Prospective students are ushered across thresholds by people who go out of their way to help them understand.

It suits me best not to require students to line up on the playground and be walked to the room. I like them to come to class when they arrive at school, straggling in individually, in pairs, or in small groups. It helps me to be able to greet and attend to students one by one so that I can read their dispositions and, when needed, sort out briefly with them what they need to work on and how they think the day might take shape. When students file past me en masse at the threshold, things get off to an all too rapid start for my liking.

Just as there are rites for entering the classroom, there are transition rites for leaving the classroom and entering the outside world. The rite can be as simple as lining up and filing out. Some teachers of young children stand at the threshold of the classroom and exchange hugs with each of their students. Others touch students on the shoulders and wish them well. The importance of the rite is that it keeps the two worlds straight. Schools are not everyday in their approach to life; if they were, there would be no reason for their being. They have specialized functions to perform, and the content, patterns of responding, symbols, and relationships are in alignment with their goals. It is because the experience of the learning community is unique that students are surprised when they see their teacher in the grocery store, and parents take special note when they see their child's teacher at a night club!

Competency Rites.   The second transition rite I observe is the rite that accompanies the passage from one state of competence to another. Van Gennup takes note of the rites that celebrate the transition from one life situation to another (e.g., betrothal, marriage, pregnancy, parenthood, occupational change). In the learning community, rites mark the changes in a student's level of competence.

Rites of competence are celebrations that intensify an event's significance or emphasizes its noteworthiness. It is one thing to set a student in an author's chair and celebrate the writing of his or her poem, but it is quite another if the celebration gives recognition to the fact that in writing the poem the student underwent a significant change in competence as a writer.

This type of rite is important to both the individual and the group. It ensures that the writer and his or her mates take note and pay attention to something that holds value. And it is not an everyday event. A competency rite should be used only at times when an achievement holds great importance in a student's development. Just as a family gives special attention to children when they enter school, and the community dignifies the passing from middle school to high school with ceremony and certificate, the learning community develops its own rites of passage. Community members go out of their way to acknowledge the new competence of a classmate. The recognition is in keeping with what the parents, relatives, and friends do when they acknowledge change of status in a young person who has had a bar or bas mitzvah, obtained a driver's license, or been accepted to college.

The following illustration of a transition rite requires background to get the full effect. Audree Miller started her career teaching English, at mid-year. In a report on her work she wrote that she found her ninth graders "sincerely wanting and in need of, a secure environment where risk-taking and differences of thought are encouraged; yet, their peer pressure and desire to be accepted in a group was so strong that they easily neglect their own unique individual differences." Students were quick to judge each other, their writing, and the literature they studied as "lame" or "boring." Audree found that getting students to expand their thinking and to get beyond the comments of lame and boring was a challenge that required getting students to be open to interpretations by others. She worked with students to make a community where trust existed and the place was relaxed, secure, open, honest, and encouraging. She worked with her students to make a place, a community, that "nurtured thinkers, trusting and willing thinkers, who valued their own interpretations, those of others, and finally re-negotiated interpretations."

Audree acted to ensure that her attitudes and behavior clearly modeled to the students what she was aiming for. She writes, "In addition to what my attitudes and behavior do display there are important traits they don't display, such as: insincere or false praise, (acceptance and encouragement, yes) or condescending remarks or ridicule. Never are put downs or attacks allowed. Certainly, supportive debate and discussion are encouraged, but simply no attacking of the character, or thoughts or interpretations, of an individual are accepted." Ways Audree and her students worked towards the building of community included:

1. Reading to the group to create a shared experience
2. Studying literature in a way that emphasized the value of both accepting and challenging the ideas of others, plus renegotiating and valuing interpretations

3. Highlighting birthdays and special occasions once a month
4. Posting notes, ideas, information, want ads, and notices on the class bulletin board
5. Conducting a writing workshop that emphasized conferencing, trusting self-knowledge, stretching and taking risks, respect, and valuing of rituals, such as mini-lessons, author's chair, and graduation
6. Holding a graduation exercise that recognized students' achievement and was respected and valued by the students

Here is the transition rite developed by Audree to clarify what was of value and to separate students from their past as writers by celebrating their newly achieved level of competence.

> Every second week on Wednesday a graduation is performed. Anticipation, excitement, and respect invariably precedes the celebrated graduation ceremony. There is even a type of reverence that permeates the air. Simply put, graduation is the honoring of each student and their final draft of a hard-worked piece. I play "Pomp and Circumstance" on the tape player, and call each student (one by one) to come up. I receive the student's final draft and he or she selects a donut and a pen or pencil and sits down to look over the piece before sharing it with the class. When students read their work, they are greeted with applause. An important key, I have found, is to not call the names too fast. I give each student time to take "the walk" and be a celebrated author.

Rites are serious business and require judgment. The rite Audree conducted with her students succeeded first of all because the students recognized that the writers and their pieces merited special attention. Students' growth was recognized. Also, the symbols selected to acknowledge achievement ("Pomp and Circumstance," pen or pencil, and food) were appropriate for the group.

All rites must be used with care, since they point the way others might take in their efforts to grow. But transition rites in particular should be used with care. A symbolic acknowledgment of change in status signals to the entire community what should be valued. A writer can write pieces that delight the community and deserve celebration. But that does not mean that the piece demonstrates a change in the writer's competence.

Overused rite will lose its significance. What is marked by a rite should be clearly of value.

Incorporation Rites

The strength of a learning community is the ability of the members to accept one another as they are and to help one another make changes they value. Members of the community choose for themselves and others, take action and reflect on the results, enjoy being with others, and express themselves willingly in a variety of ways. The persistent challenge for teachers is to create a place where members not only come together but also tolerate multiple perspectives. Members of the community need to be at home with themselves and others; they need to feel secure in not pretending to be anyone but themselves.

Here again caring is the thread used to weave cooperation, self-esteem, and growth of individuals and the group. I know teachers who have developed a rite to initiate new students into their classes. One I like is giving a couple of students the responsibility of setting up a place for the new student (which at times means hunting up the custodian to get a desk), and assigning two students to interview the new arrival. Later a class meeting is called where the newcomer is introduced and students tell what they will do to help out their new classmate in the weeks ahead. The rite closes with the teacher welcoming the student and presenting him or her with a notebook and a pen or pencil that symbolize acceptance and membership in the group. This kind of incorporation rite not only helps the newcomer but contributes to the community coming together and keeping together.

Bringing about a sense of unity and belonging is never easy—it has to be worked at day in and day out. The hardest time, of course, is during the beginning of the year when everyone is new. I think of Estes's book *One Hundred Dresses*. It's a wonderful story that gives us a firsthand look at a child from the other side of town, one who is never accepted by her classmates. Too late, the children become aware of the riches she had to offer. It's not surprising that this book is a favorite of teachers to read early in the year.

Many of us recall living in classrooms where we were too timid to respond or speak out, even when we knew the answer the teacher was looking for. How much better it would have been to have been a member of a community where risk taking was encouraged and failure was viewed as an accepted part of learning. How much better to have been a part of a group that undertook projects that required collaboration and where meaning was negotiated, rather than trying to think of the right answer.

Human beings are social in every aspect of their being, including learning. Eighth grade language arts teacher Judy Sadowsky found that she changed the social climate for the better in her room by putting a couch and bean bag chairs in one part of the room. It became the place where people shared their thoughts and feelings, as well as their writing. Judy starts the year off by sharing her writing with her students and letting them know that they are in a safe place. It is a safe place to take risks and to talk about what it is that is important to them. Should it happen that a member of the group experiences a difficult time, such as a family member dying, the group gathers in the couch area and shares.

Holistic learning requires a kind of caring that comes with a sense of belonging. Creating unity is central to community life, and teachers work at it in numerous ways. I think of my own teaching when Van Gennep writes that the rite of eating and drinking together is clearly a rite of incorporation. He sees the sharing of food as constituting a bond, and so do I. When I teach classes that meet after school, I rely on food and the conversation that goes with it to help bring us together as a group. Teachers need food after a long day of work, but more is nourished than our bodies when we share our snacks. Conversation is always richest around the food table. I had never thought of it as a rite before, but I knew that it was more than an activity. Sharing food strengthens our capacity for caring for ourselves and our ideas.

A friend once asked if there was a relationship between the quality of the food we share and the quality of learning that goes on, and I'm inclined to say that indeed there is. It is no wonder that food is such an important part of classroom celebrations. Too, I have always experienced a special spirit in classrooms where from time to time there is cooking. Of course, teachers who know the value cooking and sharing food has for community life are forced to justify it in their lesson plans by administrators who have no sense of the importance it holds for the social life of the community.

It is also important to me to have singing, movement activities, and choral reading early in the year. I think of these activities as incorporation rites. A lot more is going on than merely learning dances and songs. Play brings acceptance; physical contact is important. Both contribute to the bonding of the group. Working together, collaborating, negotiating, and giving your all is strengthened when there is a genuine affection between people and group identity exists.

Belonging, caring and acceptance are fragile aspects of learning community life and require constant attention. The arrival of two or three new students in a two week period of time can raise havoc with a solid, caring, and responsive community. Teachers who may be experts at creating community at the beginning of the school year may be far less adept at incorporating newcomers as they arrive at the threshold during the year, admission slip in hand. When newcomers arrive in twos and threes, the threads that make up the fabric of the community can begin to stretch and break. How well I remember a boy who brought confusion to a solid community for two weeks before he was incorporated into the group. He couldn't settle into his work. He roamed about the room, seldom passed up an opportunity to push and shove, and refused to respect other people's property. I needed a rite that would open the group to him and help him enter. When students are kept at their desks and teachers work their way through commercial materials, newcomers can of course be assigned a seat, handed the materials, and given assignments. It isn't necessary to teach children to collaborate, to create a union with others, and to be personally responsible for one's actions, but is the resulting lifelessness worth it?

Separation Rites

If the coming together of a group is important, it only stands to reason that the day in the spring when people take leave of one another calls for special attention. How many of us, after a year of belonging to a special group, have seen the unity begin to fall apart as students bickered and squabbled for no apparent reason? It was my friend Mary Glover who pointed out to me that our class on making holistic learning communities gave a good deal of thought to constructing and sustaining community life but had never given a thought to how to bring about a year-end closure that had the right feeling. I don't have an ideal solution yet; it's one I need to work on by listening to how other teachers deal with it, and I need to learn from them. There is a strong feeling of loss. An entry from Kathy

Egawa's notebook captures one child's feeling of loss. Erin sat with the rest of the class and stared. And stared. Suddenly she blurted out "IT'S NOT FAIR!!! IT'S JUST NOT FAIR!!!" "What Erin?" "THAT ALL THIS IS OVER! IT'S NOT FAIR!!!" I laughed—a little. But I knew exactly what she meant. So she stayed a few minutes. She stared some more and we hugged. Then she left."

Barbara Johnston has an original way to symbolically come to grips with separation. During the final week of the school year, students write a letter to the person that will be occupying their desk the following year. In the letter they introduce themselves and recount their year. Students tell about what they enjoyed, their struggles and triumphs. Class members take delight in hearing the letters that will be left for the desk's next occupant. Then on the last day of school Barbara and her students gather for the final rite. Balloons are filled with water. Once the balloons are ready the students line up and one by one take their place before Barbara. Congratulations are given and Barbara breaks a water balloon over each student's head! The school year is over. The learning community is brought to its end.

Libby Gilmore joins with her middle school students during the first week of school to anticipate the final week. Students make a time capsule that reflects their likes, dislikes, interests, and hopes for the future. The time capsules are then stored in a box and put on a shelf at the back of the classroom in clear view. During the final days of school the time capsules are opened and in general students marvel at the changes that have taken place. The event is a time for reflection, acknowledging changes, and anticipating the future.

Karen Lashley has a special way of ending the year. From time to time during the school year, Karen's group has candlelight lunches. They sit together in the dim light, eating their sandwiches and telling stories to each other. During the final week of school they hold their last candlelight lunch, which is spaghetti instead of sandwiches. This time the group members reflect on their year together and share what they will remember most about the year. What students have to say often reflects the importance of the community life they have shared, such as "I learned to cherish people."

Other teachers I know celebrate the ending of the year with pool parties and trips. But I favor the rites that pull the group together for a final time and give symbolic order to the feelings of separation. Learning communities that have historians who record the important events that happen each day can culminate the year by having each student read an entry that held importance to them. Each reading calls forth memories from others that are shared. Another kind of history is to create "life-books"—scrapbooks that students and teacher fill with pictures of themselves doing activities together in class or on field trips, snippets of things they've written and drawn during the year, and the like. This idea is good because it provides something concrete that pulls everything together. As students collect favored pieces of writing, drawings, and photographs of projects and class activities, they know what they are working toward.

Another time when there is a need for a separation rite is when a student moves and has to leave classmates behind. Susan Sullivan shared with me a rite that she used when a child was leaving the group. She would gather the students together and tell them about their classmate that would be leaving them. Next, she would read to the class Byrd Baylor's book *Everybody Needs A Rock*. When the story was finished, a small dish filled with attractive rocks was passed to the person leaving and she or he would select a rock to keep. The stone was then passed from student to student. While holding the stone, students would share something they planned to remember about their classmate or make a wish for her. Lisa Bickley and her group have a separation rite worked out for when a member leaves their fourth grade community. The group makes a circle and the student leaving sits in the center. One by one the students reflect on the experiences they have shared together. Particular attention is given to where the student has made growth and what is likable and admirable about the student. Keep in mind that as important as such rites are for the individual leaving, they are equally important for the group. The group is strengthened by caring in formal ways that incorporate symbolic acts.

Separation rites are a familiar part of today's life. Airports are wonderful places to observe different groups and cultures approach separation. In the bar, pairs and small groups have a final drink together; at gates, people exchange ritual statements like "Have a good flight," "We'll miss you," or "I love you"; others exchange gifts or tokens of remembrance; and (what I delight in seeing) children line up to get their ritual kiss from their grandmother, uncle, or other family member. Staying connected to people and places in a society in which people constantly come and go requires meaningful separation rites.

2

Celebration

The social life of the learning community is incomplete if it doesn't include celebration, festivity, and fantasy. All these are integral parts of the human experience. Harvey Cox (1969) sees human beings as being essentially festive and fanciful and by their very nature creatures who not only work and think, but who sing, dance, pray, tell stories, and celebrate. In our lives we look forward to holiday, neighborhood, and family celebrations, and we are quick to give ourselves to spur-of-the-moment celebrations. Whether we celebrate for two minutes, a day, or a week, we seek to join with others in lifting the spirit and fellowship of the group.

Schooling that is dominated by sober habits and efficiency fails to draw on the benefits that can be gained from playful and imaginative expression fostered by celebration. When we celebrate in the learning community, we recognize that people have the power to incorporate the joys and achievements of other people into their lives. Celebration not only dignifies the lives of individuals and the group, it contributes to a sense of belonging.

Celebrations in the learning community can be organized into four types: special day, spur-of-the-moment, achievement, and getting older celebrations.

Special Day Celebrations

Merrymaking and carefree enjoyment characterize this type of celebration. Routines, schedules, and work-a-day concerns are pushed to the side, community taboos are relaxed, and togetherness ranks above utilitarian acts. The mood is festive. It's a time to sing, to dance, to share poetry, and to dress up in colorful and unusual ways. At times, the classroom is decorated and furniture rearranged to allow for movement.

Special day celebrations can be part of festivities that occur outside the classroom, or they can be rooted within the life of the learning community. Halloween, Valentine's Day, Presidents' Day, and April Fool's Day provide excellent opportunities for generating festivity. Each learning community has its own rhyme and reason, and celebrating events like the First Day of Spring, Poetry Power Day, One Hundred Days of School, Backward Day, and The Final Day of School Day, which originate in each community, can also encourage fetivity.

Celebrations require planning and preparation. Whether students write poetry, make symbols, prepare rituals, make banners, practice songs, make costumes, construct scenes, write speeches, prepare skits, or work on dances, the preparation nurtures anticipation and brings everyone together.

Backward Day is one of my favorite celebrations. With the right preparation, it can be delightfully festive. During this celebration, the teacher becomes a student and the least likely of students becomes the teacher. Class leaders give up their roles to others who never take the lead. Everyone backs into the class, and the day works its way forward in as many backward ways as possible. I recall the delight I felt when Steve, who never tied his shoes, came backward through the door with his shoes tied. It is a chance for the student labeled a "troublemaker" to try out being a responsible member of the community. (And for the student who never misbehaves to make trouble for others.) During Backward Day, community members work out a plan that frees them of the rules, roles, schedules, and conventions that govern their daily lives and are taken so seriously. It is time of joyful nonsense.

What is to be gained by playing, merrymaking, dressing up, taking the role of another, and generally engaging in foolishness? First of all there is joyful affirmation of life. Next people can experience one another in fresh and imaginative ways not anticipated. This is what I have found to be true. Surely a day filled with joy and surprise and enriched fellowship are reasons enough!

The special day celebrations I'm talking about are *not* mere parties where students dress up, sit quietly in their appointed places, and have candy and cupcakes passed around to them while they listen to a story. A celebration is more than a party. For example, if the spirit of Halloween is to come alive, you need more than merrymakers dressed as witches. You need convincing witches who cackle, move, and dance like witches. A Halloween mood cannot be coaxed into being by merely lowering the lights and setting about jack-o-lanterns. It is through studying how the Halloween tradition has evolved, making up rituals and poems, chants and dances, music and oaths, that the classroom can be transformed by the authentic spirit of Halloween. The celebration is strengthened when students immerse themselves in the celebration and give way to their feelings. It is by giving yourself unselfconsciously to the moment that the worth of a celebration can be experienced.

Spur-of-the-Moment Celebrations

Some celebrations don't require advance planning and preparation. They happen spontaneously when events such as the first warm day of spring occur. Everyone gets warm-weather fever, and the celebratory response is to take the group skipping and running, and leaping and falling, to the park or playground to cavort about. During the four years I taught intermediate-aged children in New York City, I always looked forward to the first snow, hoping it would happen during the school day. There was certain to be students in the class who came from countries where it didn't snow, and they looked forward to the occasion with great anticipation. When it did happen, most of us would follow the newcomers' lead and run outdoors with mouths open in order to catch the flakes. It did wonders for our morale.

When a rainstorm becomes a deluge, you have another occasion to celebrate. A great storm summons everyone to the windows and gives one reason to bring out poetry that captures the sound and feeling of the day. It can also inspire students to read nonfiction books in order to understand what has happened, but that is not its primary purpose.

The reason for a spur-of-the-moment celebration is to release the spirited way celebrants give of themselves in response to the forces of nature. Once the moment has passed, Byrd Baylor's book *I'm in Charge of Celebrations* is a must-read, because of the inspiring way it captures the spirit of celebrating life and nature.

Once a celebration passes, it is a time for teachers and students to reflect and tell stories about other times that events elicited a spontaneous response. The experience brings the group together, strengthening bonds.

Achievement Celebrations

Achievement celebrations, when students grow in their competence, are central to the learning community. Also called an "I Am Learning," they acknowledge that a classmate, group, or the entire community has accomplished something noteworthy. While achievement celebrations lack an exuberant display of movement, sound, color, and festivity, they are nonetheless true to the spirit of saying yes to life.

Celebrations whose purpose is to recognize success cannot be truly appreciated by outsiders. Only members of a community who live closely together can weigh the significance of such an event. Feelings of happiness, respect, and sometimes even awe flow through the group. Students might respond to the achievement by clapping, offering words of encouragement, or even silence. The joy and happiness expressed acknowledges both the person or group as well as the ability of all human beings to create and make meaning.

To illustrate, Andrea, who after a great struggle masters long division when once the task seemed impossible, is celebrated. Or Jimmy manages after great effort on his part to learn to read; Jane, after numerous attempts, is elected class president; the class gets a good report from the music teacher; Becky composes a poem that brings a response of absolute stillness when it is read; Donna resolutely handles a snake even though she is white with fear; a class play is a great success; Nicky repeatedly and inexplicably gets startling results with pinhole cameras. It is the wondrous spirit that moved in Becky and that made the poem come to life that is celebrated. So it is with Donna—what is celebrated here is the fact that we can all transcend our fears and grow from them. *What we celebrate in others we can find in ourselves.* Such recognition makes achievement possible in all of us; we relive the celebrated events in the days ahead.

Teachers in holistic learning communities pay attention to their students and celebrate breakthroughs and achievements by drawing attention to what is accomplished. A kindergarten or first-grade child who invents his or her way into writing or breaks code in reading might not even be aware of the achievement until the teacher puts it in the spotlight. The same goes for a reluctant middle-school reader who for the first time finds a book he loves and reads twenty-nine pages in one sitting without even realizing it, or another who begins punctuating her usual run-on sentences without instruction. Saying "Hurray, you did it" bolsters both the individual and the group; everyone moves a bit closer together when one person succeeds.

Celebrations that recognize achievement need not last long. Usually there is a break in the flow of classroom events, and recognition is paid to the student and the achievement. "Author's chair" is one way that a student's writing can be celebrated in primary, intermediate, and high school. A chair is placed in a particular place in the classroom, and writers who have moved ahead in their writing and have prepared something for the group sit in it when they share their work. The chair symbolizes having achieved. Students gather around the author, who reads his or her piece to the group. When a student in Linda Sheppard's kindergarten sets his or her journal aside and begins to write a book, Linda draws attention to the fact and reads the opening sentence after saying, "Here is his first sentence." The celebration is short but it nonetheless sets the writer's efforts apart from others for a brief time and acknowledges the growth that has occurred. The length of time spent is not as important as the dignity with which the event is treated. After the smiles and applause, the flow of community continues.

Getting Older Celebrations

Children and adolescents want people to notice that they're growing and getting older, although with adolescents we must be careful to not pay *too* much attention—they have their own ways of celebrating the changes they go through, and public attention can be agonizing to them. Yet they do want us to acknowledge that they're getting taller or gaining access to social independence in new ways. Community life is strengthened by celebrating growth in ways they find acceptable.

Celebrations of growth recognize events as diverse as getting a drivers license and loosing the first tooth, becoming an older brother or sister and joining clubs. Each is a sign of growth. In celebrating one student's growth, the physical development that everyone experiences is celebrated. When I taught on the Yukon River, there were two boys who wore their older brothers' shoes to school one day. They tested out the feeling of being as big as their brothers. Again, celebration acknowledges and says yes to the wonders of life.

Choosing When to Celebrate

We need to keep a few guidelines in mind when we think about celebrating. A celebration has to be about some "thing" that is valued by the members of the community. And celebration cannot occur too frequently. Cox (1969) suggests that it is essential for celebration to be juxtaposed. This means that it must display contrast and be noticeably different from everyday life. Overused celebration becomes flat and doesn't contribute to the social life of the community. Therefore it's necessary that celebrations be sufficiently infrequent so that the student might both anticipate the arrival of scheduled celebrations and be joyfully surprised by those that come into existence at the spur of the moment. In prompting celebrations that acknowledge nature, growth, achievement, and success, we're celebrating a value we want to establish. That which holds value for individual and community life is celebrated.

The social relationships and history of the group are enriched through celebration—thereby strengthening the social life of the learning community—when members incorporate the joys and achievements of other community members into their lives. Celebration is perhaps our finest way of caring for others. There is a selflessness that is expressed through celebration. The other person is the focus of our attention, and we are one with them as we celebrate.

3

Conversation

*I*n everyday life, talk is the primary medium for learning, and for that reason, talk is an essential part of learning community life. There are different kinds of talk, of course, and each has its own benefits. In this chapter, I am primarily concerned with conversation as a particular kind of talk. One way to bring definition to an idea is to tell what it isn't. Therefore, I am going to tell about three kinds of talk that are close neighbors of conversation. They are caring talk, story talk, and discussion. Later, in Part II, dialogue, yet another kind of talk, will receive attention.

Caring Talk

Caring talk is an indispensable part of life in the learning community. It is friendly in tone and signals acceptance and a willingness to belong. Through caring talk, community members show concern and greet and acknowledge one another. Talk of this sort is valued because it helps maintain a shared reality and nurtures a feeling of belonging. Teachers know they have a problem when they sight a student who doesn't participate in caring talk. We all need others to accept us for who we are; we are strengthened when others welcome us and recognize our efforts. Through caring talk people in the learning community, students and teachers, learn about one another and grow in their ability to attend to one another. Caring talk is of course woven within conversation, but conversation includes many voices other than the voice of care.

At times teachers take charge of talk that has as its primary emphasis the expression of care. In Diana's class, a girl who didn't have any close friends in the group and rarely had anything to say in group activities, shared with emotion that her father had been hit by a car while crossing the street and was in the hospital. The children responded with questions about what happened, expressing sincere concern for both the girl and her father. For the first time in the class the child felt the empathy of other children in the class, and her classmates, through their expression of care, began to see the child in a new light. The event effected a change in the child's status in the class. Moreover, the event contributed to group solidarity. The expression of care strengthens all people involved and the community as a whole.

Early in my teaching career I was surprised that students came to school when there was a death in the family or a serious accident. I believe it is because life in the learning community is set apart from daily living. It is a safe place, there is a predictability to life, and students can be certain that they will be cared for by their classmates and teacher. At such times, the door is closed to visitors. Heartfelt responses are made as community members recall difficult times in their lives and how they coped. Not only is the person at the center of the care giving helped, but everyone experiences a sense of belonging, as well as something of the fragility of life.

Perhaps one important reason why we fail to make effective learning communities in our teaching is that we do not see the importance of attending to experiences our students undergo in their living. We stick to the books. Restricting what happens in the classroom to *the* curriculum tells students that their *lived* experiences do not count. The process of schooling is considered to be enough in itself. This narrow focus denies the importance of caring and the contributions social relationships can make to learning. Being in place, belonging, is not merely a feeling we have but it expresses foremostly our relationships with others who truly care for us. Genuine caring responds to the person and what is important in his or her life. A characteristic of holistic teaching-learning is that feeling and emotions are not shelved.

Talk Story

When talking about story with friends in Hawaii they shared that they had a long tradition of getting together to talk story. In my experience that is usually what happens when friends get together, but what delighted me was stating the purpose for getting together as just that—to talk story. When I thought about it, I realized that I knew teachers who pulled their students together—usually first thing in the morning—to talk story. In these learning communities, when they talk story the intent is not to develop ideas that will later be grist for the writing mill or to develop oral expression. The intent is to experience the presence of one another, to listen and enter into the ordinary and extraordinary story worlds that are made. We come to know the other person, child or adult, through the stories he or she shares with us. There is a coming together when people in a learning community intertwine the events happening in their lives through story.

Discussion

Discussion has a good deal in common with conversation, but it differs in significant ways. In discussion, students always focus their attention on some "thing" in order to know and understand. Judgments are made, ideas are reflected upon, points are debated, propositions are proven, and conclusions are sought. A discussion is usually directed toward achieving an outcome of some sort, and it frequently has a purpose that can be stated in so many words. A person (or moderator) may be in charge in order to keep the discussion on its intended track. Students share and defend their opinions, and if the going is good, students grow in their understanding of the necessary world of things, actions, ideas, and operations. It is usually possible to judge how successful a discussion has been by determining whether the anticipated outcome was achieved. It is even possible to weigh individuals' contributions by judging their effort, attitude, and the significance of their contribution to the discussion. At the end of a discussion it is reasonable to ask "Who helped you the most in today's discussion?"

The school day is filled with discussions. Discussion is an important way through which knowledge is uncovered and understanding gained about all subjects of study. Discussion might be held between as few as two people or include the entire class. In classrooms where the activity is controlled by commerical materials and the teacher giving directions, discussions are infrequent. That is because there is nothing to discuss when the "right" response is known in advance. But, in learning communities where students are empowered to think for themselves and have a voice in their learning, discussion of topics of study abound.

Conversation

As important as caring talk and discussion are to life and learning in the community, they cannot match the contributions of conversation when it comes to strengthening a community's social fabric. Caring talk and discussion can occur between strangers, but a good conversation can only come to life between people who take delight in each other's presence. Conversation is what Oakeshott (1959) calls an "unrehearsed intellectual adventure."

As a form of talk, conversation is poorly suited for providing information of a particular sort or being productive in any predetermined way. That is not to say that participants in a conversation won't learn something, gain insight into a problem, or try out "new" ways of viewing the world. It's just that we enter into a conversation specifically for the delight of it. There is no "thing" to be given specific attention; there is no purpose beyond the lively participation and enjoyment of those involved. Oakeshott (1959) believes the excellence of conversation springs from a tension between seriousness and playfulness; each voice represents a serious engagement in the conversation, upon which the impetus of the conversation is dependent. The participants as play fellows are moved "not by belief in the evanescence of imperfection, but only by their loyalty and affection for one another" (14). A conversation can last long into the night, or, when delight ceases, it can come to an abrupt halt without regard for the amount of time it has lasted. Participants are moved by the spirit of the conversation and take delight in the flow of sounds, feelings, and images they experience. If one voice becomes instructive or seeks to dominate other voices, the conversational spirit lags. While it is possible for one voice to speak louder than others from time to time, a person who insists on dominating will kill the conversational spirit. As Oakenshott notes, passages of argumentation are commonplace in conversation, but the voice of conversation itself is not argumentative. In the dynamics of conversation, one has her opinion, the other has his opinion, and both are right.

In keeping with the idea that conversation is an unrehearsed intellectual adventure significance lies neither in winning nor in losing but in *wagering*. Participants are not engaged in an enquiry or a debate; there is no 'truth' to be discovered, no proposition to be proved, no conclusion sought. They are not concerned to inform, to persuade, or to refute one another (Oakenshott 1959). The image Oakenshott presents is one of thoughts of different species taking wing and playing round one another, responding to each other's movements, and provoking one another to fresh exertion. Ideas come and go and nobody asks where they have come from or on what authority they are present; nobody cares what will become of them when they have played their part.

The learning community benefits when people speak out from their own life experiences and world views. When students speak authentically of what they know and imagine, others experience the speakers. Entering into another person's life by taking delight in their imaginative responses and through what they are willing to disclose about themselves is one of the joys of belonging to a community of caring people. It strengthens the social relationships within the community. Conversation requires a willingness to give of oneself and to receive from others. To truly understand another person, we cannot stick to the facts of what has been said in so many words. We must open ourselves to the full presence of the other person and the meaning they will into their expression. Conversation is a medium through which students learn to care for others and to be cared for. And much is possible when you are a part of a group that cares about you. To develop the social bonds in the learning community, teachers are challenged to position students with others in such ways that they increase the circle of people with whom they find it enjoyable to converse. The task is to help students identify with others and be interested in what they're thinking and doing. In middle grades, where cliques exist, the challenge can be great. The problem is one of nurturing tolerance for other people. The learning community is a temporary place. Tolerance and acceptance within the community are values of the highest priority.

Krista Sekeres remembers a teacher who knew how to bring students together through conversation. "I once had a teacher who devoted the entire first week of classes to sharing in his students' lives. We started by talking about our recent summer vacations, then shared our class schedules, then talked about our families, our future plans, our pets, our boyfriends and girlfriends, our fears. By the end of the week we were sharing our dreams, our aspirations, our lives. It was hard to believe how much we were willing to say in such a short time. He never pressured us to talk or even asked us to say more. We wanted to get close to the people that we would spend the rest of the year with. We felt comfortable, well-known, and loved in our classroom. And it never failed to amaze us that he would remember our stories and our lives years later."

Learning communities above all are safe places where members can take risks and develop their expressive abilities. Safe means that no one is to be made fun of. In conversation, we seek to join with others in fellowship. If a student is made overly conscious of his or her speaking, it is certain to interfere with his or her participation. I am not suggesting that teachers be indifferent to inadequacies that may exist in a student's speaking—how we speak is very much a part of who we are, and we as teachers are called upon to do all we can to help students be as clear in their speaking as they are able. When a person's way of talking is made fun of, the person is rejected and possibly humiliated. In the learning community, tolerance of different dialects and speech habits must be the rule.

America is made up of a rich tapestry of cultures and dialects. American English is not a language of a single correctness. I see the teaching responsibility as three-fold. First, teachers emphasize tolerance of one another's speech and create interest in how we differ yet still manage to communicate. Second, teachers work to help students broaden their ways of speaking. Students will speak in the dialect of their family and neighborhood. In school, students have opportunities to practice standard or school English. The point here is that students need not unlearn speaking that is appropriate for one situation in order to learn another. Third, teachers work to help students to be sensitive to the need to match the "right" speech habits to different situations. Any habit of speech students have is appropriate in some situation, or they would not not have acquired the speech in the first place. The language of the classroom differs from the speech of the playground, just as the talk between two friends in the backyard differs from how the same two will express themselves in a faculty meeting. We all adjust our speech to take into account situations, topics, and who is participating.

But to gain versatility the student needs opportunities to practice and use language. Conversational activity must encourage students to speak their meaning. It is not a time for calling some usages incorrect or for examining their appropriateness. Students must feel they belong and be confident that they have something of worth to offer others. Everyone need not participate in the same way—voices differ. We participate when we listen and advance the conversation through our interest. With few exceptions, children come to school experienced in conversation. They have been surrounded by it throughout life. And the majority will be quick to converse when the opportunity arises if the situation is supportive. When students are secure, conversation happens with ease and accompanies most activities that are not dependent upon deep concentration. Conversation helps ensure that each student will be able to take risks and trust both their intuition and reason to guide them.

When students have the opportunity to practice conversation, they learn how to attune themselves to the spirit expressed. They become sensitive to the effect their participation will have on others. They learn to disagree without commanding center stage or causing the conversation to collapse into argument. Through experience in conversation we learn how to enter into the thoughts of another person and to experience more than is expressed in the skin of speech.

When teachers converse with students, we should try to be sensitive to ensuring that our contributions don't carry undue weight and dominate the conversation. Conversations are fragile and don't lend themselves to manipulation by the teacher or anyone else, regardless of how well intended the motive. To help students improve their ability to converse, teachers bring students together in situations in which conversation might flourish. Shy students are positioned so that they can discover their voice and come to realize they have contributions to make. One way and another, teachers support participation and nurture a willingness to be open fully to the presence of the others involved. Students who are willing and able to give themselves to conversation can be counted on to speak out of the landscape of their experience, giving voice to their thoughts and feelings as they learn about selections of the world's meaning.

Conversation is central to community making. To give yourself in conversation to another person is to accept them on their own terms and to listen with the heart as well as the ear. Caring for one another is the rule of community life. It is a value that is fundamental. Since with caring comes the acceptance of responsibility, it is not unusual for students to hold back. A friend who teaches in junior high school explains to her students that the learning community is a temporary situation, not a life-long commitment, and that the learning made possible by caring makes it worth the effort. Caring for the other person's thoughts and feelings in conversation contributes to learning community life. Through conversation we learn who the other person is and how we might respond to him or her.

4

Play

*H*olistic teachers see play as a way for students to make cognitive, social, and emotional growth. Play enriches the imagination, provides opportunities for developing originality, and strengthens the individual's ability to cope with problems and the unexpected. Play is an essential element in community life. High school students as well as kindergartners enjoy play, and teachers have long punctuated the schedule with a times of relaxation when the spirit is encouraged to be playful. The community pulse is strengthened as students share in a playful spirit as they collaborate in purposeful work.

It was my good fortune to visit Mary Glover's learning community on a day when students were at play developing elaborate, three-dimensional board games. The activity had gone on for two weeks, and the enthusiasm was still high. I doubt that the children saw themselves as engaging in play, but the activity was imbued with a playful spirit. Moreover, students were engaged in inquiry, invention, critical thinking, argument, and dialogue. Imaginations soared as children worked on their own and collaborated in twos and threes to design games. What stood out to me was the complexity of the games—it seemed that most of the children were captivated by the increasingly complex order they created. A few of the games, in fact, became so complicated that playing them was next to impossible. Treasures, swamps, towers, moving bridges, dragons, and dungeons were numerous, and the rules were never quite equal to the questions posed and the problems encountered. To play required makers of the game and the players to collaborate. In some instances game makers became guides who negotiated rules on-the-spot with the players.

There was an immediacy to the making as children negotiated meaning and collaborated to solve problems. Learning was at its best. Mary helped children work their way through problems, make plans, organize, and pull materials together. She helped them to understand, critique, and appreciate their work, but it was the children who did work, and for their own reasons. Pleasure existed in the immediacy of the making and doing, which is a prime characteristic of play. Children were in no hurry to complete their projects. Quite the opposite. They took delight in their work and the surprises they encountered. I thought of scientists who think of their work as disciplined play and the playful feeling I experience when I am involved in building something.

Every other year, Karen Smith's learning community makes a haunted house at Halloween for the children of the entire school, their parents, and the wider community. The amount of work and learning that goes on during this time is noteworthy. Scenes have to be constructed, which requires making designs, gathering materials, and organizing work plans. Taking care to get the right sounds and appropriate lighting, inviting classes, and arranging for the movement of people through the haunted house are but a few of the problems that the community members must solve. There is a playful spirit as students collaborate to solve problems, test out their plans, and try again when they are found wanting. When the spirit of play gives way to arguments, the group pulls together, sorts out problems, and then gets back to work. Whether writing a story, building a castle, or making a haunted house, the work goes ever so much easier when the spirit of doing is playful.

Play is a matter of the heart as well as of actually doing something. Play ceases to be play if it becomes a task, because it requires a sphere of freedom and a spontaneous internal response. "Teacher, Billy won't play right!" signals that Billy is not entering into play in a playful spirit. It takes more than a crown perched on a child's head to make her a queen. She must feel queenly, and others must be willing to believe, for the time being, that she is a queen. Seriousness doesn't conflict with play. Quite the contrary. In fact, play is next to impossible if the participants do not give of themselves wholeheartedly. Involvement is what counts. To illustrate, let us look at an example of a different order.

Play in the learning community isn't all of a kind. It can be divided first of all on the basis of whether the play is what Guttman (1978) calls "complete within itself" or whether there is instead a goal to be reached outside the immediacy of the "lived" participation. The difference between play that takes the form of painting a picture or playing ring-around-the-rosie and playing a game of checkers or kickball is that there is no winner or loser in painting or dancing around hand-in-hand in a circle and falling down. Playing is an end in itself. In checkers or kickball, the intent of the players is to score and win. When activities are complete within themselves, there is nothing to prove and there is expectation beyond joining in the moment in enjoyable ways.

Playfulness is not always visible. A characteristic of expressive activities that have a playful character is that the person is immersed in the activity. There is no clock watching as students lose themselves in composing a poem, working on a group science project, solving an equation, dialoging about a book, or painting a picture. When bells announce that time is up, everyone is startled that it has passed so quickly. There is an expressive quality that guides students' work when the playful spirit is alive. Students who choose to write set themselves up in a comfortable place for writing and share what they compose from time to time with friends. Young children gather around a book and work at making meaning, pulled by the delight of making connections between the squiggles and sounds. Writers give themselves wholeheartedly to their projects. At the science table, students lift the magnifying lenses and peer for minutes on end at the insect collection, soaking in nature's structure, usually with no intent of doing more than marveling at the spider's web or sketching the butterfly's wing. Block builders are immersed in creating towers and submarines. And they post signs "DO NT TUCH" in hopes that it will keep other builders from wrecking their work to get materials to build their own machines and buildings.

Let's be realistic. Supporting playful activity and creating opportunities for people to express themselves is work. All expressive activities require that space and materials be organized, time for practice, perceptive critique if students are to further develop, and a valuing climate that is supportive of spontaneity and innovation. Major projects that involve the entire learning community, such as studying the effects of different room designs on life and learning under the guidance of an architect, as Ginny Perenza's sixth grade class did, puts demands on the group to develop organizational skills, as well as the ability to collaborate, negotiate meaning, and solve problems as a group.

Nurturing the spirit of play is challenging. Yet whether we teach kindergarten or ninth grade, we must learn to nourish the playful spirit if the learner's imagination is to be unleashed. Play, like celebration and conversation, fosters imaginative responses. Students who take a playful stance are the ones most likely to come up with original interpretations that will pull their learning ahead. By working together, teachers and students can create an atmosphere that will enable students to be at ease, confident, and secure in the situation in order to give themselves to play. It doesn't matter if the playful spirit is expressed in writing, dancing, interpreting a text, solving a problem scientifically, or organizing data collected in a cultural study—if a student is overly concerned about doing well, or if he or she feels unreasonable pressure to perform, something is lost. It is not unusual for teachers of gifted middle school students to complain that the students are overly concerned with being correct and hesitant to take risks necessary for growth. Undue concern with correctness, in the initial phases of a piece of work, blocks the spirit of play and stifles the imagination.

Teachers can encourage a playful spirit by expressing themselves joyfully, engaging in exaggerated and playful gestures, being ready to give new interpretations to the mundane, and taking delight in original expression. The straight-faced, overly serious teacher who is never willing to take part in nonsense sets a somber tone that strangles the playful spirit and is seldom effective in today's schools. Play is the rhyme that balances and strengthens reason.

Play is a double-edged sword. It can contribute significantly to social, emotional, and intellectual life of students, but it can also be troublesome and disrupt classroom life if it gets out of hand. Some students aren't content to let the spirit of play merge into their work—they want full-blown play without regard for the activity. It reminds me of my own children, when they were young, standing on chairs to do the dishes. The playful spirit at times dominated the purpose of the task, and we ended up having to mop the floor after the dishes were done.

Disorder that brings confusion can seldom be allowed, and the teacher needs to be swift in establishing order. The teaching challenge is to help the community abide by limits. There is real art in getting the "right" playful spirit for a particular situation, and teachers continually have to balance the strengths and problems that come with it. Noise that is discordant is perhaps the best indicator that the playful spirit is slipping out of control. Play is not problem-free, but when it is right, there's no doubt that it enriches life and learning in the community.

5

Routines and Jobs

Routines and jobs, more mundane and ordinary than other elements in the learning community, are nonetheless necessary if the living space is to be kept orderly and if students are to have ready access to tools for learning. There has to be a plan for taking care of the physical environment, including all the stuff students haul to school. Coats have to be hung up without confusion, lunch sacks and book bags stored so that people don't trip over them. Materials should have an assigned place, and once used, they should be returned to the spot where they belong. (I am constantly amazed at how teachers of younger children imagine ways to organize materials for easy access.) The physical space of the classroom must allow for orderly work spaces and movement. Not only does the floor have to remain uncluttered and tabletops kept clear, but chairs, desks, tables, and other furniture need to be kept orderly to facilitate the coming and going of students. The list could go on and on.

With the exception of a few students, it's usually not easy for even the most experienced teachers to bring students to "want" to care for the classroom environment. Not only do procedures that will ensure the existence of an orderly place need to be worked out, but the valuing of order has to be established. Otherwise, it's the teacher's problem. If identifying what needs to be done, working out reasonable work procedures, and deciding on who will do what and when sounds simple, think again! Except for the youngest students, few students come to school looking forward to doing their part in carrying out jobs and routines.

This problem is not just a classroom problem, either. It's also a home problem. In fact, family life can and does break down because deciding who is responsible for home routines and jobs cannot be worked out to everyone's satisfaction. The question of who is going to do the necessary work, meaning work that draws attention when it is left undone, has to be answered. Life in holistic learning communities is complex, and routines and jobs must be effectively executed. There is no choice. It is difficult for students to be responsible for their learning if the learning place is cluttered and disorganized.

One characteristic distinguishes routines from jobs. A routine implements an action designed to achieve a specific outcome as efficiently as possible. Ideally, we don't think about routines. We *do* them, on time, as needed, without a fuss. Limited judgment is involved. Students enter their room and hang up their coats, attendance is recorded and sent off to the office, notices for parents are handed out, and candy sale money is collected and counted. If routines are effectively carried out, no one will trip over boots in the closet area, paper will be passed out efficiently, and students involved in special classes and activities, such as band, will get away on cue, all without a hitch.

Initially, selecting routines requires judgment, but once they have been decided, the emphasis is on doing them. Practice is necessary to get things well established.

Jobs, on the other hand, require students to exercise judgment in carrying them out. There are always choices to be made, and jobs can always be improved upon. I cannot recall a class that I taught that ever got the problems of caring for paints, brushes, paper, scissors, crayons, and the like in the art area worked out to everyone's satisfaction. And yet if there were going to be a special visitor, or if the room had to be spic-and-span before a celebration could get underway, the jobs seemed to get miraculously done, without complaints!

With jobs, there is not only a question of when to do a job, but how. For example, the routine of checking books in and out of the library is a first do this, then do that proposition. But keeping the community library in working order is a job, just as keeping animal cages clean is a job. Not only do the shelves have to be kept organized, but the cataloging system has to be in appropriate order and the atmosphere pleasant.

Jobs offer learning opportunities that can provide occasions for problem solving, collaboration, and working together. Unlike routines, which are aimed at efficiency, jobs enable students to take charge, to organize who does what and make judgments about the effectiveness of their work. Jobs help students contribute to the quality of life in the learning community as well as negotiate meaning, take on responsibility, and contribute in significant ways to advancing a cooperative way of life.

I have always liked jobs because students can take charge of them on their own. Students of any age can make jobs the responsibility of the community government. Students decide what needs to be done, assign roles and responsibilities, and see to it the work is accomplished. It is common practice in younger grades to post lists of jobs and the students responsible for doing them. Whether teaching younger or older children, I favor creating a community government that takes on the responsibility for getting the jobs done. It's important work and an opportunity to collaborate with others. There is so much to be learned. My responsibility as a teacher is to help students reflect on their work and to arrange opportunities for them to evaluate how well they're doing.

It is poor use of the teacher's time and effort to assume responsibility for jobs and routines. If students aren't good at doing them, it is up to the teacher to help students perceive the value of the work, practice doing it, and receive feedback from the group. In taking charge of identifying what jobs need to be done, planning and doing them, and evaluating results, students use language in authentic situations to accomplish important work. That is, more is accomplished than getting the jobs done.

The contributions routines and jobs make to life and learning in the community cannot be overemphasized. When a large number of people share a crowded place, productive life is possible only when the place is orderly. Routines and jobs are a necessary part of community life.

6

Residency

When I think of ritual, rite, ceremony, celebration, play, and conversation, I think of a procession. The root of the word "procession" is *ced*. It means to yield, to give way, to turn aside, to go back, and that is the way all of the elements above work. When I'm teaching, I find it helpful to think of the primary function of these elements as making a *residence* for students. Residency amounts to getting a roof over everybody, making public as well as private places for dwelling. In creating residency, teachers and students seek to ensure that members of the community are *centered*—that they have confidence in themselves and others and that they feel at home. Individuals are in residence when they feel at ease in expressing what they think and how they feel, in taking risks, and in seeking out critique of their work in an effort to grow. Students in residence express self-esteem, can take the initiative in learning, are able to trust themselves and others, and, perhaps most important, experience their existence as being of value to others.

When teachers join with students to make a learning community, they have two broad goals in mind: first, they want to make a place that challenges students intellectually, and second, they want students to value learning and be up to the challenge. The second goal is connected to the first. If students are to engage in serious study and work hard at developing their interpretive and expressive abilities, they'll need to be self-confident, capable of collaborating and negotiating meaning with others, and willing to cope with the failure that is certain to accompany the kind of learning that pulls students beyond the familiar. The elements we've discussed so far are weighted on the side of the second goal. They are not used expressly to bring about learning, interpret a piece of literature, or to learn how to write, but to make a place for students, to bring them together, and to nurture their willingness to give their all to learning and to reach out and support others in their efforts to learn.

In making a residence for a student, the teacher works with both the group and the individual. The process is circular: as the group comes together, the individual is strengthened, and as individuals grow in confidence and expression, they increase their caring contributions to the group. Although caring for the group is a concern for holistic teachers throughout the school year, it is most important early on. Each learning community is a very small society, and there is the ever-present danger that it will become small-minded, petty, and restrictive. Students might experience a sense of not being wanted by others, especially when school is just getting underway. Teachers therefore do all they can to help students realize right away that making a friendly, supportive place where all community members can reach out and connect to one another is of utmost importance. Caring relationships are central to residency. To begin, there must be community activities that build the sense of oneness.

Activities that require classmates to pull together to accomplish something worth celebrating helps. If group members are to belong one-to-the-other, then something must be made that can be valued by everyone. Some teachers organize science projects or drama activities that require students to collaborate. One teacher I know began the year for her fifth graders by calling upon them to organize a field trip. I like the idea of getting out a class book during the first week or doing something that needs to be done for the school. Whatever the activity, what counts is that in making something of value, students not only learn something about the world but they also begin to recognize that they have something to contribute and appreciate others for who they are and what they might offer.

Touching, too, is important. It communicates personal acceptance. I'm moved by how easily young children reach out and take the hand of newcomers to give them a tour of the classroom, show them where the lavatory is, and take them to the playground. Appropriate touching says, "I like you. I want you to feel that you belong." Ceremonies in which students join hands and sing while opening or closing the day strengthen bonds.

And we must not underestimate the power of words. Students should not be left to fill in the blanks about how teachers feel about them—they need teachers to respond verbally to something they've accomplished, some action they've taken, or something they've said. Here are some examples:

"Just look at these paintings."

"Our class is going to know more about how our community is organized and how the government works than any other group in the school."

"Morag is the very best fixer we have, whether it's with equipment or people. Just look at what she did to keep this group going."

"I have never worked with a group that can organize such good plays so early in the year."

"Mark is certain to be a poet. Listen to what he just wrote."

Valuing that leads positively to the future is singled out. Confirming what is and imagining what might be clears the way for students to take on values, trust their budding competence, and renew faith in themselves and the group. And although the teacher's good words are essential, they're not enough. Other members of the community need to voice the message of worthiness. That means that the students must do or make something their mates consider to be of value. At times, this is a challenge. Early in the year, teachers may have to dig deep to uncover what it is that a child has to offer. But as long as the teacher makes it clear to students that all in the community have a responsibility to be accepting of others, a secure atmosphere begins to be established.

In an interview with five members of a fifth–sixth grade learning community Karen Smith made with students, I asked what they would recommend to teachers who wanted to start the school year by bringing students together and forming a community. Since all of the students lived in the same neighborhood, I was surprised by the way they emphasized the importance of students getting to know one another. They also proposed that on the first day, students undertake group projects so that they could learn to work together. They suggested what they called "new games" that required people to touch and cooperate. They also proposed that a student government be worked out as soon as possible, and that the teachers read stories like *Crow Boy* and *Johnny Tremain*, stories that Karen Smith had read and that emphasized cooperation and valuing one another. The learning community is a place that stands apart from other fields of meaning, and values must quickly be established. These students pointed out that learning to work together and growing in appreciation of one another was of foremost importance.

My teaching partners agree that literature is an important vehicle for creating residency. Times for sharing literature are embedded in ceremony, ritual, and celebration. Maureen Carpenter speaks of the members of her learning community as sharing common bonds that are anchored in the story worlds. She puts it this way, "Each day as we read and talk about books that reveal our own lives, we will also be valuing each other and our ever-changing and expanding universe."

There is no particular method or way to establish residency. More important, one cannot assume that once residency is established, it is set for the school year. We all lose our footing at times. So, too, can students lose their place, their sense of worth, their membership in the community. When this happens, something has to be done to create a place for the person. Social relationships and the caring ways of community members make residency. Students are encouraged to participate in group life by joining with others in conversation and play, ceremony and celebration, routines and chores, rituals, rites, and ceremonies. Teachers initiate joint activities that involve making plans and taking action. They nurture caring responses, for caring for others is the heart of residency. Students are helped to see that in caring for the welfare of others their own being experiences care. In short, teachers act on the knowledge that learning is social as well as cognitive.

Teachers cannot create residency on their own. Community members need to recognize their interdependence and consent to enter into a co-operative way of learning. If even a small group of students refuses to give its consent, the community will suffer. In fact, one or two students can undermine community spirit. Teach long enough, and even the best community builders will encounter students who refuse to aspire to group values and repulse efforts to bring them into caring relationships with others. Worked with individually, the students might be just fine, but they will balk at giving something of themselves for the welfare of the group.

There is no guarantee that teachers and their students will be successful at making a learning community, instilling necessary values, connecting people, and establishing residency. Some classes simply will not come together and care for one another in ways that strengthen living. Try as they might, teachers when confronted with such a class find themselves unable to exercise the authority needed to pull the group together. The group is all important where community and residency are concerned because it is within the group that values are established. If the group will not consent to form a web of caring relationships, teachers have little choice but to be technicians and individualize instruction. It's unfortunate, but all we can do is try our best.

Students in residence are confident that others will be there for them when needed. They know that they are capable of contributing to the lives of others by generating ideas, helping solve problems, making things that others value, and enjoying the presence of others. A student cannot be expected to have confidence and be up to the challenges of effective living and learning if others do not value his or her presence and contributions. Like it or not, we depend on others for seeing our lives as meaningful and being of worth. It is hard to imagine being able to experience yourself as a friend if no one else thinks of you as a friend, or as being intelligent if others don't value your ideas.

A kindergartner in Linda Sheppard's class was hesitant and lacking in confidence. In a conference, the student's father spoke with pride that his son knew all of his tools by name and helped him in his work by getting tools for him as he needed them. The next day the teacher made the point of talking to the child about what his father had said and how smart she thought he was. The child beamed. Later in the day, he came to her and whispered, "Tell the class." The child knew something about how to help make a residence for himself in the learning community. If you doubt the importance of others knowing you as a competent, intelligent being, listen to the stories you tell others about yourself.

Elizabeth Sewell (1964) writes about caring and the dependency of humans upon one another. Sewell takes the position that it's the work of each person to care for the well being of others. "The work of being human begins with the human being as soon as he is born, and lasts a lifetime. It is the main occupation and travail of our early years, but it never ceases as long as we are alive. . . . We have to work on ourselves, and other people work at or on us: our family, our teachers, our friends, the society to which we belong. . . . We work at and on them, too" (15–16). The image Sewell develops is that of a web made up of the whole human world, individual and communal, in a constant state of making and remaking, in a process of self-construction. The processional elements are directed at creating a web of caring that makes a place for the group and the individual. The experience that is lived by participating in rituals, rites, celebrations, and play often exists beyond the words we have.

Making Sense
of Experience

*I*f the elements we've discussed so far have been *processional*, the elements we are going to discuss now can be thought of as *progressional*. The movement is not circular but forward. Parade, critique, and dialogue operate to bring students to encounters with the world for the purpose of learning about it. Students encounter ideas, objects, problems, and situations that require them to be reflective and come to grips with the world in alert and thoughtful ways. The idea behind parading, critique, and dialogue is to effect learning by helping students to make a project of some selection of the world's meaning. The intent is to challenge students' thinking and to disrupt the tranquility of idleness and certitude whenever it occurs.

In making a place where students belong, the emphasis is on lived meaning, keeping the group together and establishing residency. Progressional elements, on the other hand, shape activities that involve students in learning about the world, and making a project of it. By project I mean that students take up selections of the world's meaning—subject matter to be understood—to make sense of their experience and construct meaning. Processional and progressional elements are interdependent. Together they make a place where students can work confidently at making and critiquing meaning.

The teacher's orientation in conducting progressional activities is to ensure that students are self-projects who take the initiative, make choices, and engage in critique. Students who are self-projects work at understanding what they are doing, seek out connection within their experience, and judge their work and the work of others with an idea of how the object of critique might be improved. Students are responsible for posing problems, constructing meaning, and raising questions. A ready-made world is not handed over to them.

Before exploring parading, critiquing, and dialogue, a few words need be said about how teachers working from a holistic perspective view language. It is the teacher's orientation to language that breathes life into situations created for learning about the world. After a brief orientation to ways language is put to work by students in their learning encounters, I will examine how parading, critique, and dialogue bring students to encounters with the world for the purpose of making a project of it.

7

Putting Language to Work

The learning community is a language environment. Students undergo experiences that place demands on their understanding, and they come to grips with those experiences through language. And because language maintains its usefulness—does not become an object of study—language competence is gained while learning about the world. From this perspective learning is the result of an interplay between the learner and the "other."

In order to make sense of the world, students have no choice but to draw on who they are and what they know. We are all connected to the world and we are each the center of our knowing. A person's background, life experiences, and culture contribute to both the content and shape of the meaning he or she expresses. Because we are so talented in our construction of meaning, we are seldom conscious of our contributions to the meaning-making process. Traditional orientations to schooling downplay the importance of social contexts and consider knowledge to exist independent of the person who seeks to know. Holistic teachers accept that people are intentionally connected to the world and view learning as a conscious search for creating unity and making sense of experience.

Learning communities outfit students for:

- Using language to learn about the world's meaning

- Enjoying the presence of others and working together

- Posing problems, undertaking projects, and seeking a "new" perspective on perplexing questions

- Improving upon existing situations by exercising critique

People learn language to participate more fully in the social life of family and community, not for the sake of learning language. Language and learning are both social. It is by using language to learn and to participate in the world that understanding of language and the world develops. "As in language learning, learning in general occurs in social contexts and is mediated by others. Even learning in private, by oneself, counts as learning in a social context since it taps into meanings and memories that have been socially formed" (Edelsky, Altwerger, Flores 1991).

Numerous studies have been conducted in recent decades on how young people learn about the world and express what it is that they know. Foremost of these studies is one reported by Gordon Wells in *The Meaning Makers* (1986). These studies have helped illuminate how teachers might align learning in school with how young people learn in their homes and neighborhoods. The studies can be used as a foundation for approaching speaking, writing, and reading as *processes* for learning about the world, *not* as content to be learned. In daily life the essence of language, its usefulness, is what is maintained.

What follows are a few ideas about language and learning that I find are an integral part of learning activity. They emphasize (1) the importance of students thinking for themselves and (2) students conducting their study of selections of the world's meaning from a critical perspective. These are foundational ideas when learning and teaching are conducted by means of parading, critique, and dialogue.

Approximation

In matters of learning, both adults and children achieve competence over time. Learning that counts takes time and effort. Previously much has been made of readiness activities, the idea being that students develop prescribed skills before they get down to doing actual work. Over the years children have surely consumed a ton of paste in cut-and-paste activities that supposedly helped them in their readiness to learn to read. We have not been willing to look at what children can actually do.

From a holistic perspective, the concept of getting students *ready* to read, to write a critical essay, or conduct a science experiment doesn't make sense. Human beings are born *ready* to learn. We have a gift for making sense of life's happenings. Whether students are learning to write, express meaning in mathematical terms, or interpret a literary text, the first step is to get them busy doing what it is that they want to do. Teachers attend to how the students work so that they can help them along. Not everyone has the insight required to appreciate the potential for learning that exists in the resulting scribbles, the faulty equations, and the mediocre interpretations of literature. But it is what the student can do. With constructive feedback and practice, results will improve.

Unfortunately, traditional schooling based on fake learning exercises and textbook drills more often than not hides what the student can actually do. Neither talent nor inability can shine through these regimens. That is why it makes sense to get on with the work, get started. What students need is feedback on how they are doing and encouragement when their way of working shows promise. Students' work, what it is they actually do, is critiqued in order to help them see possibilities for developing meaning. When something does not show promise, something has to be done. At times the only choice is to start again. But both student and teacher will be a bit wiser.

It is the way of holistic teachers to study how a student works at learning so that the way of working can be made visible to the student and alternatives proposed when needed. Holistic teachers call on students to engage in "real" work and stand up to the results. When you think about it, it is a coward's way to push students through learning exercises that do not require them to do their own thinking and work. A teacher will never find out what a student can do if the student is required only to memorize or complete someone else's thoughts. Students can work their way through a four-foot stack of English exercise books and never learn how to write effectively.

Central to the concept of approximation is the idea that here is no single standard of correctness. Teachers pay attention to the direction students' work is taking, their effort to make meaning, and their intent to express meaning. Increasingly valuable outcomes occur as teachers and students attend to what has been made in the light of what *might be*. The process of learning and the results or product are reciprocal. An improved way of working will bring about better results. The process is viewed as a product in the making. Undue emphasis on results, the product, independent of the making does as much harm as good.

Some people would argue that this is the long way to go about bringing about results and that it is ever so much easier to focus on the correct response and teach students how to produce it. My response is that for lasting results, the long way is the best. The tyranny of correctness in the name of efficiency has resulted in dull classrooms and mediocre learning. Products are important, but teaching that emphasizes exactitude uproots students by not allowing them to do the work themselves. It is easy to teach students correct responses and how to arrive at them, but is the resulting knowing of value? The world is a complex place. Schools are good places for students to practice thinking, to get good at viewing events from multiple perspectives, and to learn how to learn.

Opportunity

It's become cliche that we learn to speak by speaking, read by reading, and write by writing, but it is nonetheless true. Learning, whether it involves critiquing a political decision made by the president or predicting the weather, requires practice informed by knowledgeable criticism. Opportunities to work at what is to be learned, coupled with feedback from someone who knows the territory, facilitates learning. To become good at anything, a person must work at it, and for some of us it takes a good deal more work than others.

Learning has its best chance when students have plenty of time to work on ideas and projects in situations where there are others (teachers and fellow students) to help them attend to details and to sort out what is significant. This is the way learning occurs in families. Teachers are at fault who call on students to work without providing them feedback on how they are doing. All too often in clock-ruled teaching, students jump from one subject to another without allowing time for them to come to grips with the meaning it is hoped they will learn. Learning that is not hinged to giving thought to what has been undertaken is not likely to be any more productive than is sitting around thinking about what might be done without taking action. This is where large classes hinder learning. Of course, teachers can call upon students to share interpretations, taking time to talk about what happened and its meaning, before ending a class period or activity. Writing in learning logs is another way to slow down the action and to initiate contemplation of the significance of what happened. But these are poor substitutes for having the teacher consciously attend to what has happened and guide students in making their own critical assessment.

Collaboration

Learning benefits when partners co-produce meaning. Ideas get a better workout. No one truly learns in a vacuum. Students need informed feedback on how they are doing and an audience that will appreciate their efforts as well as their results. Nothing is more destructive in education than competitiveness. By that I mean the three reading groups, the standardized test scores, and the talk of being above and below grade level. Self-esteem is essential to learning. There is reason to do everything possible to insure each student succeeds, whatever the age of the student. Why should classrooms exist where more emphasis is placed on who got what score and who is ahead and who is behind than on the honest to goodness effort made at learning?

In holistic communities, when learning can be advanced by moving alongside students and joining with them in the learning activity, teachers see no reason to hesitate. Learning goes best when teachers follow the student's lead and ensure that the student's thoughts are heard. The teacher can compensate for what a student knows and doesn't know by simplifying, paraphrasing, and putting meaning into contexts that are familiar to the student. Together, teachers and students collaborate at making meaning.

Traditional schooling gives little importance to collaboration and the importance of others, perhaps owing to the faulty view that cooperation is always the enemy of individualism. Today, however, we are beginning to see that where language and learning are concerned, other people are important. People depend on the social body, the community, in every respect for their existence. Being together with others in a place outfitted for learning enhances opportunities for students to encounter the world in interesting, complex, and critical ways. It is through contact with others that meaning becomes intelligible to us. It is through our encounters with others that we determine what is of value. And, perhaps most important, we do not merely need the services of others but we need others for themselves. Togetherness is the fundamental value of our existence, and within this togetherness all other values can assert themselves (Kwant 1965).

There is an advantage to having people with different interests, backgrounds, and experiences work together to achieve a common outcome. It helps them learn to live and work together. When students collaborate, they expand their choices and opportunities for action. Joining students with different interests and abilities to work on a project increases learning opportunities. Each student brings a personal way of working, a desire to know, and knowledge. I continue to be amazed by the learning and caring that results when teachers of young children and older children get together and pair learning buddies. Students of different ages care for one another, work, and learn together for an hour or two a week. If you have not tried it, don't think for a minute that it is only the younger student who benefits. Not true.

Negotiation of Meaning

Teachers and parents of teenagers are quick to learn that life is best when they don't dominate over the teens but negotiate meaning. By negotiation, I don't mean compromise. I mean understanding the other person's meaning. We all benefit when others give our ideas serious attention. Through negotiation, students come to understand how someone else interprets an event, text, or situation; thereby, the basis for their own understanding is broadened. Too, they have an opportunity to see how another person goes about thinking through a situation or problem. Negotiations in the classroom, since they are face-to-face, provide ideal circumstances for students to get feedback on whether they are being understood and to improve their communication accordingly. When meaning is negotiated, people sometimes change their minds, but that's not the primary purpose. Meaning is negotiated to ensure that we understand one another's point of view and meaning.

Feedback

Developing attitudes, acquiring values, developing skill, and coming to know requires that students have opportunities to work with content and learn how they're doing. We all benefit from the insight of others who are knowledgeable about what we're undertaking. Therefore, teachers must not only organize learning encounters to ensure that students get feedback, but they must become expert at providing critique, disclosing meaning, and helping students see how they are doing.

Feedback is not always the result of reasoning. There are times when we are likely to say "I feel that . . . " Feedback is more useful, however, when it is supported by knowledge as well as informed by feeling. Feedback that has the best chance of pointing the way to further growth makes clear to students what it is in their work that holds promise for development. A young child working at writing needs more than a pat on the back and statements such as "Oh, such good work." The child is helped by drawing attention to what she or he has accomplished. A student who conducts a science experiment and receives only a grade for his or her work is cheated of gaining insight into what it was that made the project noteworthy. It is the work of the teacher to help students to "see" what it was that they did, to illuminate what is unique and significant about their work. The work of the teacher as it is with all critics is to disclose meaning and the potential for making meaning that would otherwise go unnoticed.

Appreciation

Appreciating a person and what it is he or she can do is an important way for teachers and students to promote growth. When people are genuinely valued for what they do, their self-esteem is strengthened and they are encouraged to grow. Being attentive to others and, when the moment is right, celebrating achievements contributes to students' development.

It is very difficult, if not impossible, to learn in a situation where the learner and his or her work are not appreciated. In education, it is ever so easy to focus on what it is a student does not know. What counts, however, is what the student *does* know, for you cannot build on what is not there. Paying attention to what it is that students can do and appreciating them for who they are is not only sensible from a teaching point of view, it is also fair. Describing students by labeling them "culturally disadvantaged" or "children at risk" amounts to judging others by what it is that they don't have, don't know, and don't do. And who is to set the standards and do the judging? Whose culture is the correct culture? Holistic teaching seeks to appreciate students for who they are and what it is that they can do.

An orientation that values the foregoing ideas is essential for making the most of the ideas to be discussed in the next three chapters. Parading, critique, and dialogue bring students into contact with the world in ways that call upon them to collaborate, negotiate meaning, give one another feedback, and show appreciation. These behaviors can be learned, and it is unreasonable to expect that students will be good at them without having an opportunity to practice. Be patient. Value and study the approximations students make. Let the student be the informant about what to do next.

The going will be hardest early in the school year. It takes time to learn about one another. It is hard to hear another person's meaning until you know something about him or her. As the teacher's knowledge of the students increases and students get to know one another, compensating for what one another knows and doesn't know becomes easier.

1st 6 wks

8

Parading: Leading and Following

When people with varying abilities act in leader-follower relationships with one another, they are parading. I became aware of parading in my daily living before I saw it in my teaching and in the teaching of others. The first time I took note of it was when my family lived in Kaltag, Alaska, a village on the Yukon River, where my wife, Georgia, and I taught children aged from five to fifteen. One afternoon in late spring, a game was being played with a stick and ball. What caught my eye was that the youngest children, instead of standing apart watching, were involved in the game at one level of play while the older children played at another. Encouraged by the older children, the little kids played intensely and actively, and they experienced the spirit of the game fully. It was joyful to watch them. They didn't yet have the skills of catching, throwing, and hitting the ball, but nonetheless, they experienced the essence of playing the game. In fact, they felt they were the center of the game, unaware that it was being played at a level beyond their participation.

A few years later, I taught in New York City. One day, I took a group of kids to watch the Ringling Brothers Circus parade through Central Park on its way to Madison Square Garden. My idea was to watch the parade as it assembled at the north end of the park and watch it as it got underway. The parade started, and much to my surprise, the kids went with it. Mark and Ross went with the band; Kim and Lisa marched alongside the big cats. David joined the clowns. And so it went. Not content to stand by and watch the parade, the children joined it from the inside to experience it as best they could. There was nothing left for me but to run to a point ahead of the parade and collect them as they passed!

Parading is not to be confused with giving a demonstration, although the two might be thought of as close cousins. In teaching, when a demonstration is given, a certain amount of distance exists. We show how something works; we illustrate the way of performing a particular act. At the end of the demonstration, we ask, "Do you understand?" There is something to be learned, but the structure of a demonstration does not involve participants in actively expressing meaning. In a parade, the spirit of doing is all important. Paraders are involved in making, doing, performing. As a teacher, I stand apart and observe a parade and have the opportunity to observe students as they work with content. I have a chance to judge what students know and their ways of working to improve their competence.

People of all ages learn by parading alongside or behind others who know either a bit or a lot more than they do about an activity. Parade leaders set the tone and show the way. Followers join and give themselves to the experience, participating as the spirit and interest moves them. In parading, there are no fixed models of behavior to be reproduced or standards to be met. Paraders join freely, out of interest, and continue to participate as long as the situation allows. When their interest lags, they drop out of the parade, perhaps to work alone.

For example, when working with microscopes for the first time in the school year, I take care that the microscopes; materials for making slides;

and paper, pencils, and colored pens for record keeping are readily ava___
able. The excitement begins when a couple of students set to work maki___
slides. I share my thoughts when asked, and in no time, the parade is
underway. Children with a bent for working with a microscope distinguish
themselves, and others, following their lead, practice. Parade leaders do
not necessarily always know all that much about what they're doing in the
early going. But they are willing to risk and get the activity moving. Problems surface in such real-work situations, and by solving them, students
have opportunities to grow. In parading, leaders drop out, students who
once followed take their place, and the activity goes on. When the spirit
of the activity begins to lag, it's time to sit down and give thought to what
happened, what was learned, and to lay plans for the next time out.

Here's another illustration. When teachers help young children express themselves in writing, they often organize materials (pencils and
paper, crayons, magic markers) and talk with the children about content:
what the children want to write. Teachers stir the ideas and feelings that
support students in perceiving, making connections, and taking the initiative. Students are not asked to reproduce a model or practice a particular
skill; they are encouraged to step out, to do something, make marks, communicate on paper. Students who are confident that they can make sense
on paper do step out—they take the lead. Students who are hesitant about
what to do are helped to enter into the writing alongside one of their
classmates. Teachers seek to help students into the flow of getting the
feeling of being a writer, experiencing the essence of writing, of having
something to say.

In communities where the students are experienced in literature studies, it's reasonable to expect that newcomers will have some difficulty in
participating fully at first. There is so much to know. How to enter into
and participate in the dialogue and learn the concepts and vocabulary
necessary to literature study are just a few of the challenges. It's not unusual
for these students, when they seek to know, to be encouraged to join an
experienced literature study group. What better place could there be for
experiencing what it is a literature group does? The students parade along,
supported by the interest and knowledge of others, until they catch on.

Parading acknowledges that much can be learned that cannot be cat-
egorized at a conscious level. There is an intuitive side to knowing. For
example, science isn't just about the scientific method. There is the whole

feeling of doing science, of wondering, of being curious about the world and what makes it work and having the imagination to tease out answers. The same holds true for learning about mathematics or expressing oneself in song, drama, and story. I recall a five-year-old who sat in the hall one day and cried because none of his classmates would read with him. As we shared a book, I discovered the problem. He whisked through, turning one page right after another at record speed, and capped off each reading with, "Now, wasn't that a good book?" The sounds of words and the pictures were of no real interest to him. He had not had the advantage of parading his way into story with more experienced readers.

Parading recognizes that the nonreflective and reflective parts of our being interact. People do not grasp meaning entirely through the intellect—there are tacit ways of knowing that depend on experience. In these instances, students should not be jerked into reason and asked to make statements about something outside their direct experience until after they've had a chance to become familiar with the thing. How can students be expected to express themselves originally—whether through speaking, writing, movement, painting, construction, or a project—if they have not explored meaning in thought and feeling, finding out for themselves what it is they want to say?

Holistic teachers value experiences that don't require students to consciously manipulate meaning. Leland Jacobs takes the position that you can only teach a person something that the person already knows. I interpret that as meaning that where genuine knowing is concerned, we can help people to name what is that they know and exercise increased control over it. But the knowing is something that the person must do for him or herself. Knowledge is personal and it is up to each person to make sense of his or her experience. It cannot be handed out like paper and pencils.

What we know about language acquisition and learning makes it imperative that teachers try to arrange learning encounters that allow students to take charge of their own learning. Parading increases the chance that students will be able to encounter the world on their own terms. It enables students to get a foothold and take up meaning in an active way. Ideas and actions are tried out and paraded about. Teachers position students who are unsure alongside students who are making headway. Leaders step out and parade their knowing and followers paticipate with little or no risk to themeleves.

Parading is not unique to schooling. Think of all the times in your life you have moved alongside others to follow their lead, thereby allowing you to participate in an activity where you lacked the skill and knowledge to stand on your own. Parading recognizes that meaning is socially constructed. In parading, we act on the possibility of adding ourselves to the world by following the actions of our fellow human beings. What is more, parading acknowledges that people have many sides and many possibilities to express those sides. Parading puts students in contact with knowing that transcends language. Of course, language can extend and illuminate experience, but parading is not dependent on the rationally ordered concepts. We can constitute meaning in lived expression when we are a part of the living moment. Much is possible in the way of expression once we experience the meaning with someone with whom we share a common bond.

9

Critique: Discriminating Among Values

Democratic societies put their faith in the ability of the individual and group to sort out good from bad, right from wrong, better from worse. Without people able and willing to judge for themselves, a democratic society is unthinkable. The assumption upon which democracy is based is that an informed citizenery will be able and willing to attend to facts, make distinctions, appreciate differences, and form judgments. The public's recent insistence that critical thinking be taught acknowledges that the ability to exercise critique is too important to be left to chance.

Holistic teaching emphasizes developing students' critical abilities. Where understanding is the foremost concern, critique is prized as a process for determining value, constructing meaning, and giving shape to content. By exercising their critical abilities in learning activities, students develop both their knowledge and critiquing knowhow. Making meaning and critiquing go hand-in-hand.

Critique is a part of everyday life. People are confronted daily with information about economics, politics, art, environment, and social issues that call for them to take a critical stance and make judgments. We depend on mechanics, doctors, electronic technicians, and other people who have expert knowledge to solve problems. A learning community is a place where students can work under the guidance of a knowledgeable person to develop their understanding of particular subjects and their ability to think critically about them.

Being literate means being able to make informed judgments about literary experiences, not merely report back what was read. Literacy is not the mere mastery of a collection of basic skills. Dewey (1930) noted that "He who has learned to read as we call it, to read without having learned to judge, discriminate, and choose, has given hostages of dependence to powers beyond his control. He has prepared for himself a readiness to undergo new modes of intellectual servitude" (117).

Critique is an integral part of all genuine knowing, whether in the arts, sciences, mathematics, or daily living. The ability to exercise critique requires not only that the critic have knowledge of the subject or object of study—the facts, the actual situation—but also an idea of what "it" *should be*. Kwant (1967) writes "For he must try to determine whether what *is* is as it should be. He must know, therefore, *how* that which *is* should be. The "should be" in question is generally referred to as the *norm*. For this reason we can say that critique is *the evaluation of the facts in the light of a norm"* (19). We all have areas of knowledge where we are respected for our critical ability, and other areas where we are dependent upon friends or professionals to help us out. One of the joys of learning, at any age, is the improved ability to discriminate and make perceptive judgments.

It is through critique that we humans are able to improve upon situations. To improve a situation, one must examine what *is* (what exists) and imagine how it *should be*. Improving upon a situation, a relationship, or developing a project or idea hinges in part on knowing what *ought to be.* We are truly stuck when we are in a situation that is not right—whether it's a car that won't start or an essay in need of repair—and we cannot imagine what *should be.*

Norms people hold for guidance in making judgments about *what should be, ought to be, or could be* are a product of critic's values, knowledge of the subject, their experience with it, and what it is that they value. When in need of help it makes sense to seek out a person who knows the facts, who has lived perceptively with them, and whose values you trust. Because knowledge of the subject is basic to critique, there are those who question whether children should be encouraged to engage in critique. They assert that knowledge of the facts must come first and that youngsters rarely know all the facts. People who take this position expect teachers to teach in a way that is not in keeping with how people live their daily lives. Whether or not human beings (children or adults) have adequate knowledge of the facts of a situation does not stop most of us from taking a critical stance and making judgments. The ideas arrived at, the judgments reached are not always sound. Newspapers provide a daily record of the shortcomings as well as the achievements of the world leaders and the stories we share among friends tell our own successes and failures. Life requires that people of all ages sort, judge, and choose. Not knowing all of the facts of a situation does not free us from having to make judgments. More often than not we have to act on what we know. Where students (or adults for that matter) are concerned, it is reasonable to expect their critiques to reflect their experience, knowledge, and interests. I find the young have a seemingly inborn ability to judge. They know what they like and do not like and sometimes can tell you exactly why. Just listen to young children's critiques of movies. I hasten to add, however, that although I listen with genuine interest to my five-year-old grandson's enthusiastic reports on movies he enjoys, I do not attend the movies. In fact, I make certain that I do not go! I know something about what he values in movie-going.

Teaching that centers on critique believes that all human activities have an expressive character, and a function of education is to aid students in developing their expression. There is no reality that appears to us which we do not constitute through our expressive activity (Kwant 1969). Knowledge is not looked upon as something that is there for the taking. People have no choice but to make sense of their world through their actions.

Our very lives demand that we express ourselves to experience our being. In our gardening, writing, worshiping, building, reading, playing, making friends, doing mathematics, painting, and caring for one another we express ourselves. Life calls for our active construction and expression of the world as we experience it. Teachers require students to construct meaning and to critique what it is that they and others make. Teachers also provide feedback to students on how they are doing. The foremost challenge teachers face, however, where critique is concerned is to help students to become aware of what *could be*. Students are challenged to broaden their horizons, to understand the world more deeply while remaining rooted in their own experiences and intentions.

If we accept the expressive character of human life, we can see that critique is the key element in enhancing students' expression. Instead of answering students in terms of yes or no, right or wrong, we can ask them how they can make something better, thereby drawing into the light what *ought to be* or *could be*. Holistic teachers don't see teaching as handing over knowledge. The learning is up to the students. It is up to the teacher to help students identify what it is the students hope to achieve and to help them as needed. They point out students' strengths. They encourage students to question and to observe. They nudge, pat on the back, suggest without dictating, and challenge. And, finally, they help the students critique the results of their efforts.

It sounds simple, but it isn't. Such teaching requires not only subject knowledge but also imagination, honesty, willingness to trust, and creativity. It is hardest for me, whether I'm working with a child or an adult, to critique when the student's expression is terribly inadequate. What do we do when there seems to be nothing to go on? For example, when teaching writing, all is well when students find it easy to express themselves, and it is wonderful when they are eloquent. But it can be painful when students feel themselves to be inadequate, are unwilling to risk, and refuse to truly involve themselves, to try their best. What do we do when it seems as if nothing is there to draw out?

It's tempting to resort to such fake learning techniques as having students write sentences using spelling words or completing language exercises in a grammar book. But holistic teachers cannot afford to do this because they understand that the knower and what is to be known are connected, not separate, and to resort to exercises is to undermine a student's potential as a learner. We must somehow find a way to focus on something a student knows or cares about. The subject might be art or mathematics, nature or a sport. (Mathematics has usually worked for me.) The idea is to get the students involved in doing, in expressing themselves. In the beginning, what they produce is not so important as the fact that they make something. When something is made, feedback can be given and plans for the next try considered.

A key idea is to help students understand that learning is not a passive activity, that knowledge or understanding neither exists in a book nor is the property of the teacher. How many times have you spent ten, fifteen, twenty minutes with a shy student, working to dignify his or her life and experience, helping the student to see that he or she has important ideas and experiences to share? It is often hard to convince students lacking in self-esteem that to learn you need only do the best that you can do, receive feedback on how you are doing, and to try again in the light of new possibilities. But it can be done. Learning from this point of view is a partnership. Students are not in a sink-or-swim situation. With practice and perceptive feedback, progress can be made. Self-esteem comes when students see themselves as contributors to their own knowing. It is empowering for students to realize that knowledge is personal, that the knower contributes to the making of meaning.

In our teaching, when we exercise critique and stretch our imaginations in an effort to comprehend a situation, make an interpretation, or solve a problem, we demonstrate for our students what critique is and how it can function to make sense of what is happening.

The Critiquing Cycle

The critique-centered, teaching-learning cycle consists of the following:

1. Identifying what is to be critiqued
2. Judging its worth by asking is it what it *should be*
3. Making plans for improving
4. Taking action—trying again

This is how writing is improved through conferencing, how an equation is finally solved, and how an art or science project evolves. Some "thing" that has been made is judged as to whether it's the best it could be. Once the judgment is made, an idea is shaped to bring about improvement. The plan for improvement is tested out and the results are judged once again. This is how we make progress in our lives outside of school. Why should it not be the vehicle for progress in learning and teaching? Students' progress in every area of the curriculum is the result of their improved ability to exercise critique.

When students take up an area of expression for the first time—let us say speaking about politics, dancing, designing science experiments, or writing poetry—we can expect their interpretations to be naive and under-developed. But we know that in time if students have opportunities to study and practice, if they are given perceptive feedback on how they are doing, they will develop their expression. They will grow in their understanding of what might be and in their ability to perform. It is possible to view life as undergoing constant revision, as individuals become aware of new possibilities. This is why groups are so important. Not just students, but all people need others when they are trying to grow. We need others who will appreciate and support our efforts, others who know more than we do so that what *might be* can be demonstrated, and others who have the ability to help us understand our work and ways of bringing about its development.

Critique is not a school subject; it is the way we learn. It is important that schooling that emphasizes critique values *approximation,* as does learning that goes on at home. That is to say, students involved in the process of learning how to learn, learning how to see, learning how to interpret their world are not expected only to develop "correct" or adult responses and interpretations. Students are allowed time to develop their understanding of what *could be.* They are expected to involve themselves in the content of study or in the activity of expressing themselves and to do the best they can do. The results of their efforts are then judged and possibilities for further development uncovered. Many people will not see this as an efficient way of going about learning. And I am the first to agree. But it has the advantage of not requiring students to engage in fake learning experience where they produce "right" responses but make nothing that is genuinely their own.

Opportunities for Critique

It's not only within the study of subject matter that opportunities arise for students to practice critique. For example, imagine a class that is having difficulty in cleaning up the room and in conducting an orderly dismissal at the end of the day. The teacher meets with students to think about how to solve the problem. First they take a good look at the problem and discuss it until there is a clear understanding of what the problem is. Next they hold a "what if" discussion that results in ideas of what they would like to have happen.

Teacher: Is everyone agreed that we need to find a way for us to leave the room neat yet get out orderly in time for buses? O.K. Any ideas?

Alfonso: When we stand up to leave, we clean up everything that is around us as far as we can reach.

Gary: But what about all the space left?

Annette: Let's assign everyone one of those spaces left, like the sink, the books, the math shelf. Then everyone has two spots, one around them and their special one.

The talk goes on. Once an idea of what an orderly dismissal and cleanup is worked out, it is time to organize a plan for achieving the results the students have in mind. Prior to dismissal time, the plan is tested out and judged for its effectiveness. The results, what actually happened, are judged in light of the plan, what *should have been*, and the plans are made for the next day. It takes time but the work is important. The critiquing cycle of action, reflection, planning, and acting again is continued until a satisfactory procedure is worked out. The idea is simple but it works. A community evolves in part because the group works together to accomplish something that makes life better. And in the doing students begin to take on values that are important to group life. What is more, they practice a process that will serve them when other problems arise.

Teachers can also act as critics in contexts other than the learning community. For example, when conflict exists between students and within groups, teachers can choose to respond to the problem as an occasion for engaging students in critique. Conflict at times is caused by different values and ideas about what *ought to be.* In restoring order, teachers can go beyond having students simply tell them the facts of what happened and ask them instead to identify what the behavior ought to have been, thereby making the norms of behavior the focus of attention. It is at the level of understanding norms and reaching agreement that behavior can best be influenced.

Where norms are concerned, it's important to keep in mind that we can seldom if ever spell them out in so many words. In criticism (as elsewhere), it's true that we rest finally upon the instinct and faith that underlies our reasoning. We will have some consciousness of *why* the better is better and *why* the worse is worse, but we depend upon intuition as well as an informed and discriminating mind (Dewey 1930).

As difficult as it is to clarify norms used in making judgments, that is exactly what teachers attempt to disclose. If critique is centered on discriminating among values, and growth can be marked by a changing of norms, it follows that teachers are in part concerned with making norms that are used in arriving at judgments visible. Teachers are interested in what makes up the *should be,* and they do their best to uncover what students use as a basis for their judgment. Growth is possible only with a shifting of norms, and teachers can subject existing norms to criticism. It might be the norms that guide the behavior of the group or those that underlie an editorial in a student newspaper. A persistent problem in teaching composition to young children and older students is to cope with the first-draft writers, the ones who say, "That's all I can think of" or "Here, it's done." As we struggle in ever so many ways to help students change their expectations of what their writing ought to be, we can note their progress by referring to the norms that guide their work.

It's in this way that teachers seek to draw students beyond statements of "I like" and "I don't like" in making judgments. Being aware of thoughts and feelings that form the basis for judgments can nurture intellectual and social growth. In teaching we seek to make students aware of what is being set forth—the expectations—as best we can. The challenge is to move them ahead to increased awareness of what is possible, while keeping in tune with the students' knowledge and experience. For example, one year after the Persian Gulf War, students in a seventh grade social studies class were arguing about whether or not the war was a success. Sides were formed. Both sides were making their judgments based on what they thought should be. The teacher artfully slowed the argument down, quieted the voices, and called on the different groups to clarify the reasoning behind their judgments. In the dialogue that followed over the next two class periods, norms (expectations of what ought to have been) were teased out. The argument was defused and a focused discussion of the expectations different groups held took place. The ability to determine what *is* and *is not* of value develops over time, and change in perception takes time. What counts is the teacher's awareness of the process of criticism and that judgments be based on the values people hold. "Facts" are interpreted, and how an individual or group arrives at the interpretation of those facts is what matters.

When we work to help our students to become informed and perceptive critics who examine the norms that guide their thinking, I cannot help but believe that we are serving democratic ideals. Kwant (1967) writes "The actually existing norms must be subjected to critique in the name of man's freedom. Man is rooted in his society and in his past, but he is a 'self-transcending movement' and, therefore must place himself at a distance from his own past. As a dynamic being, man may not bind himself permanently for all generations to any particular form of existence" (107).

Because changing one's perception takes time, it's important that students *remain rooted in their experience* when they engage in critique. I expect students at the beginning of the year to talk primarily about what they like and do not like about a story. Liking and not liking is important. True, such statements do not give a listener much to go on but they are rooted in the person's lived response to the story. As the year progresses, as students gain in their confidence and benefit from good teaching, their interpretations will reveal the thinking behind these feeling responses. I am disappointed in my teaching when I fail to help students bring out the thought and feeling behind the "I like" and "I don't like" statements. Whether the subject matter is literature or science, I see the teaching responsibility as one of helping students uncover words that interpret what it is that they are experiencing. Often this is difficult work because it is so easy for teachers to push their own ideas off on students, thereby distancing them from their experience. I recall an instance many years ago when I was conferencing with Becky, a wonderful writer, about a piece of her writing. I was excited about the piece she was writing and told her how I thought it should be shaped. Her response was, "That's a good idea. And when you take time to write later today, I hope you can use it."

Teachers attend lectures, take classes, and read books so that we might experience more fully what it is the world offers us. Through study we learn to discriminate among values. We learn to see more perceptively by learning what might be, by being knowledgeable about the potential for experience that might exist in a particular situation. In turn, our students benefit from our improved ability to see and to interpret our experience. I enjoy reading and know that my values concerning literature will evolve just as long as I am willing to pay attention and seek out possibilities. If I'm going to keep reading a story, there are norms that must be met by the author, and there are others I hope will be met. A basic expectation, a must for me, is that the writer has to tell about people in such a way that they come to life for me. I want real people in the stories I read and not characterizations. I want to feel the vitality of the characters. Further, I want the author to have sorted out nonessentials and focus on what is "big" to life, the essential components of human existence. I want the author to stop the fluidity of life long enough for me to be able to see it, to contemplate it, to experience it. I expect authors to help me to develop insight into situations, people, and the complex world we share. I also hope that the author is able to come to grips with what is truly significant in life—to see through the fragmentations of experience, the disjointedness of reality, and to illuminate the harmony and truth and unity possible in human experience. These expectations are high, and although they might not be met, the fact that I hold them is important to me as a reader. They keep me alert and contribute to my seeking and constructing meaning. They contribute to my appreciation of story and art of writing.

When I talk about this with students, I attempt to draw norms into the light to at least some degree so we can examine what is shaping our interpretations. I hope to model a voice of critique that is not a one-sided attempt to find fault but one that seeks to illuminate, to disclose meaning. A rule for critique in the learning community is to begin by having empathy for what the maker of the object of critique was attempting to achieve. As students take up a critical perspective, relative to their own work and the work of others, it makes all of our experiences richer. It's by learning the voice of critique that students have their best chance of not only making meaning and disclosing promising ways for becoming, but of revising meaning to more accurately express experience. A quote from John Dewey (1930) says wonderfully what the importance of critique is about:

> Creation and criticism cannot be separated because they are the rhythm of output and intake, of expiration and inspiration in our mental breath and spirit. To produce and then to see and judge what we and others have done in order that we may create again is the law of all natural activity (21).

10

Dialogue: Uniting Critique and Inquiry

*D*ialogue is a special kind of talk where learning is concerned. Dialogue is unlike conversation, where people experience the delight that comes from entertaining ideas in a context where being with others is of foremost importance. In dialogue, people are important but constructing meaning is a primary concern. Conversation is combustible and can take off in an unanticipated direction without notice. Dialogue, on the other hand, has a focus, and participants join for the purpose of understanding, disclosing, and constructing meaning. To illustrate, when a group of teachers comes together to make plans or solve a problem, it is a good bet that the place will be alive with conversation. The conversation will gradually die down when someone directs attention to the issue or problem at hand and the teachers begin to puzzle about what is involved and to attend to one another. Dialogue occurs when people share a common interest and join together to understand. Often an uncertainty exists. In dialogue we attempt to call forth the best the other person has to offer and put forth the best we can imagine. Dialogue requires thoughtful listening and responding. It is a time when participants collaborate and co-produce meaning. Where learning is concerned, I believe the kind of talk to be prized above all others is dialogue.

In dialogue we once again see the importance of social relationships to learning. Dialogue respects how people come to know. People join together, responding directly to each other and the world in an effort to make sense of something. In fact, at its best people are more than partners in dialogue, which has its best chance to flourish when it takes place between people (young and old) who care for one another. This care and trust create a social condition where participants open up and accept not only the other person's ideas, but the other person, too. Buber (1969) writes that "In genuine dialogue each of the partners, even when he stands in opposition to the other, heeds, affirms, and confirms his opponent as an existing other. Only so can conflict certainly not be eliminated from the world, but be humanly arbitrated and led toward its overcoming" (27). In dialogue, it is the calling forth of the other, a wanting to hear, that summons up the best a person has to offer.

Dialogue encompasses two qualities that are central to learning: *critique* and *inquiry*. It is dependent upon people who can rise to the challenge of paying attention and thinking critically. Listening is central because dialogue is a spontaneous, give-and-take proposition. Participants do not sit waiting for their turn to say their piece. There is no planning of what is to be said. Dialogue emerges as people call forth others and respond without forethought or plan. There is no unraveling to determine who is responsible for what, because meaning is co-produced.

It is in dialogue that students in the learning community have their best chance of discovering they have a gift for knowing. It was my good fortune to teach with Alvin Smith, who was both an outstanding artist and teacher. Alvin could stand alongside a student who had an art project in the making and through dialogue help the student to better understand what she or he was about in the making. He didn't ask questions but simply made observations about the work. When his statements were confirmed by the student or the student called his attention to something he hadn't noticed, the dialogue was initiated. Together, Alvin and the student shed light on what the student had underway. The dialogue went beyond dignifying the work to helping the student understand what he or she was coping with. I have observed much the same process followed by teachers of writing, mathematics, and science. Together, the student and the teacher make inquiries, arrive at judgments, and shape a course for future action. Dialogue is occasion for exploring norms with the student. Through dialogue, students gain insight into what might be realized in their work.

There's no question about it, making inquiries and maintaining a critical stance while working in partnership requires attentiveness to both the person and the ideas. Dialogue participants are obliged to follow the thinking of one another and to perceptively join their thinking and insight with the contributions of others. This lets ideas take on new possibilities.

Teachers who are basically educational technicians rely on materials that present a standardized view of the world. They try to motivate students to learn the material, with grades and promotion being the primary rewards. There is no student ownership. The thinking and seeing that go into the learning experiences belong to the person in authority and the developers of commercial materials. In dialogue, however, what does and does not happen is controlled by the people involved. Meaning arises from collaboration as partners respond to one another in an attempt to uncover meaning and construct an accurate representation of the subject of study. Freire (1968) asserted that dialogue cannot exist without a profound love of the world and people. He viewed love as the foundation for dialogue because love is an act of courage, a commitment to another. Partners respond to one another in an attempt to uncover meaning and construct an accurate representation of the topic or subject of study. They make inquiries and offer critiques of one another's thinking as they express their thoughts and feelings on the topic. Even unformed and naive thoughts count in dialogue because they can clear the way for others' thinking that illuminates more fully the shared concern.

As members of a dialogue group, teachers do not necessarily take a back seat. They avoid narrating what the experience is about, but they do not hold back information that will move the understanding along when they are sure of the need. Here is an example taken from Karen Smith's field notes. The literature group is studying *M.C. Higgins the Great* by Virginia Hamilton, and they are having difficulty getting into the story.

Karen: But if you're really feeling frustrated with it I don't want to make you hate reading either.

Marco: I like it except for just that one part.

Karen: Real tough?

Marco: Yeah, that was the only part.

Eppy: The only part that . . .

Marco: You lost track of . . .

Eppy: Because of yesterday how we were describing it, well then when I was, when I was comparing it to the other books, it was different because on *Let the Circle be Unbroken*, I can see everything. I can see the bushes and I can see the trees and I can see the roads, the dirt roads and everything.

Karen: Ah, huh.

Eppy: But then with this one, it's like there's nothing there it's all plain.

Sara: Trees.

Eppy: Plain like the end of Steeps and . . .

Karen: Yes, it's a different setting and the interesting thing about this book, too, is the whole story takes place in two days.

Group: TWO DAYS !!!

Karen: Two days. This is only two days in his life. Every little minute almost is given pages. That's kind of interesting when you think that an author can take two days of a person's life.

Karen listened to the students as they talked about the difficulty they were having in making sense of the story. But once she had insight into the problem they were having, she did not hesitate to supply information that would help them to make sense of the text. After all, she is a partner in the dialogue.

Dialogue plays a central role in the outstanding literature studies Karen conducts with her fifth-sixth grade class. Here is an another example of dialogue taken from the *M.C. Higgins the Great* study. Here we see students working together to understand the influence the mountain has on M.C. and his father.

Silvia: There's this part right here where it starts, "Just to remind us that she had claim to me and to you." The mountain, Sarah, owns M.C. and his father. And I think that M.C. wants to get out of there cause she . . .

Karen: You feel that ownership means he feels like a slave to Sarah?

Silvia: Sort of. Like here, "Don't be afraid," Jones said quietly. "For she not show you a vision of her. No ghost. She climbs eternal. Just to remind us that she holds claim to me and to you and to each one of us on her mountain."

Karen: Wow, read that again, that says a lot.

Silvia: "Don't you be afraid," Jones said quietly. "For she not show you a vision of her . . .

Karen: She not what?

Raul: Shows you . . .

Silvia: ". . . for she not show you a vision of her. No ghost. She climbs eternal. Just to remind us that she hold claim to me and to you and each one of us on her mountain.

Raul: Well, when I read that, I sort of thought of Sarah as head of the family, like when you said, "claim to each of them" they had a, they were representatives of Sarah and the mountain. Like if anything ever happened, they would be there to protect it. You know.

Marco: Yeah, like if someone tried to buy it, they would not let them buy it.

Raul: Like the king, he owns his guards and he holds claim to them so they have to protect it.

Karen: Unhuh.

Raul: And so, that's sort of, you know . . .

Silvia: I thought of it like Jones doesn't want to leave there cause there's protection, because she owns them.

Karen: So that's kind of the opposite.

Raul: So, she's watching over them while they are watching over her.

Silvia: Still, they're not that free, like she shows, she holds claim of them.

Karen: I really think Jones, especially, isn't free. He's never really thought things through and made decisions. He' just always had this fear almost that controls his life. The fear of Sarah, the fear of the mountain.

Raul: M.C. can feel the, like the claim that Sarah has over them because . . .

Karen: He can evaluate the mountain and be critical of it. Where his dad won't be critical at all. He won't say . . .

Raul: And one day M.C. might break that and, but the father will have a harder time breaking it but either he won't break it or he'll have a real tough time, he'll probably stay his life trying to break it. He'll die there on the mountain anyway.

Members of the group share their interpretations of the text and respond directly to one another. It is a time when a reader can get the thoughtful attention of the group to questions and problems they are having in making meaning.

It is possible to have a discussion with just about anyone, but dialogue happens best when there is a true interest in the topic and a degree of empathy exists between participants. As I've mentioned, the challenge to teachers is to build a community in which students will attend perceptively to one another and care for what the other person thinks and feels. It takes time and practice working together before adults, let alone young students, are able to attune themselves to the thinking of others. What it is that teachers say and do to nurture the development of attentive and caring attitudes can imitate or parallel what people do in their homes and in other social groups. Teachers take the lead in demonstrating caring for their students' being and ideas. They care about their students' lives, families, and what is happening to them. Effort is made to help students to take interest in one another and to value others not just for what it is that they can do but for their very being, their presence. Here is Diana Doyle's experience in starting down the dialogue path, taken from her writing about her second-grade class early in September. Diana observed:

The risk taking was still tenuous. The students leaned their bodies toward me as I read *The Selfish Giant*. When I finished the initial reading, some of the students became restless and began finding other interesting objects in the room on which to focus. Some wanted to make a connection with the book.

Sam: Why was it winter so much?

Sally: Because the kids weren't there.

Jane: My mom says this book is about Jesus.

Diana: Does your mother talk to you about the books she reads to you?

Jane: Yeah, she tells me what the book is about.

Diana: Do you have the same ideas as she has?

Jane: I don't know.

Diana: What were you thinking about when I read the book?

Jane: Well, I started thinking about Jesus but then I thought about how the giant was different in this book—you know he was mean and then he got nice.

Sally: Oh yeah, he changed from bad to good.

Diana: Wow! Think about that.

Diana observed:

> What an opening. How many ways we could go from that observation. This time we directed it to a chart of the differences in the characters of giants we had read about. Some evil, some good, and some changing. That led to other characters in books that changed. With an open ear even in the beginning of the year a teacher can find opportunities for guiding the dialogue to elements of literature. With Jane's connection between books, we were able to look at characterization in literature and establish a new way of reflecting on story.
>
> Slowly and gently we are probing one another's minds for meaning so we can reflect, rethink, and reshape our own way of looking at story. We test others' ideas against our own so they can be refined and then tenuously offer them back to the group. If these ideas are accepted and valued, we will risk again with new connections and reflections—and even the teacher takes part.

In dialogue, one person doesn't control the meaning making, but joins with others to make sense of experience. Take the following dialogue, where a group of eight-year-olds engaged in a literature study of *Stone*

Fox.. The students were working their way through the text for the first time, when they became puzzled about why the grandpa was staying in bed and refusing to get up.

Jill:	Why did the grandpa stay in bed? It doesn't make sense.
Chris:	My grandpa stayed in bed when my grandma died. He didn't want to get out of bed. He was sad.
Lee:	Sometimes I want to stay in bed.
Ms. James:	It's puzzling. I wonder why he doesn't tell his grandson what the problem is.
Chris:	Maybe it's a stroke. My grandma had a stroke.
Jill:	He's afraid to tell him. It's too scary.

The students were puzzled. They looked critically at the incident in the story and shared their thinking about why the grandpa refused to get out of bed. The dialogue was short, but the basis for comprehending the text had been broadened during the exchange. Notice how each child brought his or her own life experiences to the dialogue. They had hunches about why the grandpa stayed in bed, and the mounting tension of the story (and perhaps their dialogue) pulled them to continue.

Such dialogue is not unique to the study of literature. It happens whenever students in heartfelt collaboration seek to know, to understand. Dialogue might focus on students' working to express their own and the teacher's age in a number base other than ten. Or in making a questionnaire for polling students on a problem of concern in the school. It even happens in the block corner when children are making a foundation that will support a tower that is taller than anyone in the room.

Teachers who use dialogue with students recognize the value of working together to interpret experience. They see it as an effective way to help students see for themselves. By encouraging and supporting students' efforts to construct their own meanings and to test out the value of their thinking within the group, interpretive development is nurtured. In learning through talk—as in learning to talk—children are active constructors of their own knowledge. What they need is evidence, guidance, and support (Wells 1986).

To approach knowing through dialogue is to acknowledge that making meaning is a transactional process. Meaning originates within a dialogue and encounter, and the interplay between the learners and what commands their attention. Making meaning is transactional. Giving and accepting meaning are always inseparably connected. We interpret our experience. Genuine interpretations—not parroting someone else's meaning, or "false seeing"—reflect the intent, background, and experience of the individual engaged in making meaning. It is by sharing interpretations within a dialogue—responding directly one to the other—that opportunities arise to negotiate meaning and to broaden the base for understanding. Through imaginative, informed, and critical exchanges, partners in dialogue improve the chances that they will construct a more accurate representation of reality.

Dialogue offers an obvious alternative to schooling that outfits students with standardized views of the world and its content. Reality is viewed as a process that undergoes constant transformation. "Once it is understood that the world and the truth about the world are radically human, one is also ready to understand the statement that there is not one world-in-itself but many human worlds, corresponding to the many attitudes and standpoints of the existent subject" (Luijpen 1969, 78). People are constantly thinking, interpreting the meaning of their experience. Dialogue puts students into contact with the interpretations of others, thereby enriching the potential for comprehending their experience and understanding their world.

The voice of dialogue requires that both teacher and students take risks. A degree of uncertainty and accompanying tension can exist when teachers educate through dialogue, since no course is charted in advance. In fact, a basic rule of dialogue is that participants—teacher and students alike—do not enter the encounter with a plot in mind to be acted out. *Spontaneity is essential.* It's the immediacy of the responding, the calling forth of the other, and the listening that moves participants to insights that cannot be realized through solitary thinking. Dialogue is an alternative to making students consumers of textbook views or projects of someone else's thinking.

Since it requires inquiry and thinking critically, dialogue won't come to life if interest lags. Exercising intelligence, critique, and imagination are the essence of dialogue. When interest is strong and purpose clear, dialogue can bring about new insights as long as there are people wanting to know and willing to give themselves imaginatively to the encounter.

For example, dialogue about how a student might go about improving his or her composition will be nonproductive, no matter how well intended the teacher is, if the writer has lost interest in the piece. Of course, it is possible for the teacher to dominate the student and see to it that the work is done, but the results here will not be rewarding.

Whatever the subject of study, the idea is for the teacher to work alongside the students in an attempt to bring them to examine facts for themselves and draw their own conclusions. While negotiating meaning with students, teachers must keep in mind what the students seek to know; they can compensate for what is and isn't known as best they can in an effort to sustain inquiry. Information is supplied in accordance with what the situation requires. By listening and not overpowering their students with knowledge and intent, teachers can act collaboratively to build shared meanings that will help students construct meaning about the subject of study, meaning that reflects the students' experience and intentions. The process of coming to know can be sustained by attending thoughtfully to what is said so that they can link emerging ideas of promise to others familiar to the students making the meaning. The idea is to confirm the value of the work at hand and, when possible, to assist students in integrating what they know with emerging ideas.

The single greatest roadblock to students exercising their voices of critique and dialogue in learning is the standardized curriculum that makes a project of students, pushing them all down the same track. First, such a curriculum is unable to take into account teachers' and students' purposes, backgrounds, and interests. Second, teachers and students do not think for themselves but act out ideas drawn up by someone else. Third, the content of a standardized curriculum is packaged into numerous separate subjects. In language arts alone, for example, there is reading, spelling, language study, handwriting, speaking, and written composition. But one subject hardly gets started before it's time to shift to something else. Both the content and the day are too chopped up to organize purposeful work that involves students in thinking and acting for themselves. There are too many subjects to be covered. The school day is a mix of pieces from several puzzle boxes, and nothing fits—one textbook is finished and another is pulled into place. Pages are covered on schedule to comply with institutional requirements. There isn't time to teach, time to listen to students, time to plan with them, time to pay attention to what is important in their lives. Personal ideas, interests, experiences, and needs of students count for next to nothing—what is going to happen has been worked out in advance.

The voice of dialogue cannot exist unless teachers and students are in charge of the learning. Students cannot be expected to work collaboratively, make inquiries, or conduct observations and form judgments if they are expected to use textbook materials and act out someone else's plan. For dialogue and critique to succeed, students not only need to have knowledge, feelings, doubts, and hopes in at least some state of development about the topic being studied, but they must also have a sense of control. The voices of critique and dialogue can be heard only when participants base their responding on their experience and have a desire to understand the object of study more fully.

Wells (1986) made the following statement concerning students learning language and using language to learn: "From observations outside of school, we know that students are innately predisposed to make sense of their experience, to pose problems for themselves, and actively to search for and achieve solutions. They will continue to bring these characteristics to bear inside the school as well, provided that the tasks they engage in are ones that they have been able to make their own" (120).

Here is the challenge. How can the thinking that is common to life in the home and the community be practiced in the learning community? How can we as teachers avoid domination and seek to help students to be self-projects who come to know by making inquiries and exercising critique? Dialogue offers one possibility.

Making
Learning
Communities

When it comes to making learning communities, I believe success is hinged in two places. The first is the way authority is exercised. With dialogue, for example, students must be empowered to take the initiative and exercise authority. And, it does not matter that teachers can put to work the elements of ritual, rite, celebration, and play to make a place for students if teachers use their authority to make a project of the students rather than liberate them to take charge of their own education. The second is whether learning is conducted through real life activities. Much has been said of the importance of viewing learning and language as being social. A dynamic social existence is dependent upon students' involvement in real life activities, those that are in keeping with what happens in daily life. Authentic work activities make genuine caring for other people's ideas meaningful.

11

Authority: Empowering Students

The primary function of authority in a holistic learning community is not to control students or to require obedience, but to empower students to take the initiative, think for themselves, and assume responsibility for their own learning. Students who are empowered have the *personal* authority needed to express themselves confidently, judge their work and the work of others, and take action in their own best interest as well as the interest of others. Authority is a central issue in teaching. Teachers exercise authority—let there be no doubt about it. Learning is at best haphazard and chaotic if teachers are unable to exercise authority in their teaching. What is important is that there are many kinds of authority. Authority is a broad continuum that comprises obedience to externally created rules as well as respect for one's own ways of thinking and acting.

Teachers who want to stand on the safe side of public and faculty cluster at the obedience side of the continuum. Let's be honest. Teachers who collaborate with students and seek to empower them are sometimes looked upon by others as being (at best) naive and (at worst) foolhardy. Tongues cluck as someone in the faculty lounge reports, "Why, the kids tell *him* what to do!"

It's time to set the record straight. The word "empowerment" separates traditional teaching from holistic teaching. Simply put, *holistic teachers require students to be responsible for their own learning*. That is to say, ideas central to holism such as valuing intuition and feeling as ways of knowing, plus recognizing the importance of living and learning where social relationships are based on caring, as well as content, are made operational by students' taking responsibility for their learning. Teachers *are* responsible for caring for students the best way they know how, but the learning is up to the students. If a student refuses to put forth the initiative and think for herself, in spite of the good efforts of the fellow students and teacher, there is not much a teacher can do. Of course, we can persuade, coax, and bully students into work, but learning that results in a true change in competence will happen only when a student assumes responsibility for learning. There is no choice. Learning is personal. Others can help, but the learner has to do the work. In holistic education students are self-projects. To take this position raises questions about authority.

Authority in traditional classrooms is simple, clear, and certain. It is not open to revision. Students live and work within a fixed frame of reference that is not of their own making, where reality is defined by teachers and the textbooks and workbooks used. The teacher's authority is not open to question, and students are rewarded for following directions and doing what is "right." Rules are posted, and the teacher, credentialed by the state, serves *in loco parentis*.

This kind of authority is unacceptable in a holistic learning community, where students are required to be guided by their own thinking. The "do as I say" idea of authority is not consistent with strengthening students' ability to critique the world for themselves and to bring form to their own interpretations of experience.

Most teachers teach in bureaucratic, top-down hierarchical systems that insist on obedience. These systems are a great deterrent to learning. The irony is that superintendents and other administrators who do not do the work, who do not live in the crowded place with students, and who all too frequently have scant knowledge of teaching are the experts. They say what will be, and they insist on obedience to the curriculum and myriad regulations. Teachers in turn tell students what to do and insist on obedience.

Is there any reason to believe that obedience to authority strengthens students' intellect and enriches their imaginations? Is there any reason to believe it helps them to develop the backbone to stand up for what it is they know and believe to be right? These questions are not only important educational questions, they are critical to a democratic society.

If it is true that people have no choice but to do things themselves in order to understand, if it is true that we learn through inquiry, testing out ideas, and critiquing results, then why is obedience to other people's rules so important? Good manners are certainly necessary, as is respect and caring for others, but why *obedience*? Obedience has a low priority in holistic learning communities, except where matters of safety are concerned. Being responsible and taking initiative have high priorities. Holistic learning emphasizes the importance of developing situations that provide genuine opportunities for people to be busy with the world for the purpose of learning.

Authority in the learning community is directed toward liberation, empowerment, and supporting students in seeing and thinking for themselves. Since students are required to be responsible for their own learning, their willingness to think for themselves and to exercise control over their actions is a must. If students are to learn, they must assume responsibility for making a serious effort.

Winning students over to the idea that they must be responsible for their own learning is not always easy. Students often see the teacher's authority as absolute and think that their role in life and learning is to comply passively with authority. It is all the harder when parents believe that it is the responsibility of teachers to tell students what to do. In fact, life is easier for both teachers and students when higher-ups do the thinking. It is easier to complete someone else's thinking and act out their plan than it is to be original in your own thinking and responsible for what you do. Yet doubt, ambiguity, and struggle have a contribution to make to learning. Easy routes to learning, however, seldom (if ever) result in lasting growth.

Different Kinds of Authority

Teachers who seek to be holistic in their teaching can help students realize that authority need not be top-down. In much of life, authority is actually shared and negotiated. From a holistic orientation, authority is understood to be in a constant state of making and breaking. Authority is *misused* when one person is in charge all of the time.

The nature of the situation has a lot to say about who should take the lead and how the leader should work. It is a question of knowing what ought to be. Sometimes the teacher is not in the best position to be making such judgments. And even in those instances where the teacher knows best, his or her judgment need not prevail. After all, the students are supposed to be doing the learning. They need to test out their thinking and judge it for its worth. If teachers are going to be constantly determining what should be, when are students going to have an opportunity to develop their ability to sort out what is and is not of value?

Learning is not advanced by dominating over what it is students read and write about. Such action limits learning. For example, learning how to select and develop a topic to write about is central to writing. So is learning to select a book that is right for you from hundreds of available titles. Why shouldn't students have a say in what they are studying and the perspective from which they will work? Surely a goal of education is to free students from being dependent on the teacher. In holistic learning communities, teachers are not the only source of worthwhile ideas. Democratic values are strengthened when teacher and students view authority not as an absolute but as a process.

The emphasis on collaboration, negotiation, and joint projects requires leadership by the teacher and students. In learning communities where students take the initiative, expression is valued, and student leadership is promoted. Strengths and weaknesses in authority are made visible. Learning communities provide opportunities to study the nature of authority firsthand.

The influence authority has on learning is of foremost concern in holistic learning communities. What follows is a framework for thinking about the relationship between authority, empowerment, and learning. I find that the book *Women's Ways of Knowing* (Belenky et al. 1986) names the challenges teachers face as they seek to empower students and encourage them to assume responsibility for the meaning they make. Belenky and her colleagues discuss five categories of knowing that women have demonstrated in liberating themselves from domination. Their work shows how women's self-concepts, authority, and ways of knowing are intertwined. The women's stories show the struggles they undergo with authority as they "claim the power of their own minds." I find that the categories developed by Belenky and her colleagues can illuminate the work of holistic teachers who seek to empower their students. Education is a liberating act, and helping students overcome the domination of others is at the heart of teaching. The irony in teaching is that we who work at liberating students are ourselves at the bottom of a hierarchical system. We are handed down prescription after prescription of what to do and how to do it. Our work is to conform with the ideas of the person doing the prescribing.

1. *Silence:* People in this category see themselves as mindless, voiceless, and subject to the whims of external authority. They have little awareness of their own intellectual abilities. They do not expect anyone to listen to them. Often, they are not aware that they have a contribution to make to their knowing. External authorities are believed to know the truth and are all-powerful. In education, passive learners who are silent cause teachers the greatest concern. And no pedagogical achievement is greater than succeeding at coaxing a student out of silence and into having a say.
2. *Received knowledge:* In this category, people perceive themselves as capable of receiving—even reproducing—knowledge, but do not consider themselves capable of creating knowledge on their own. I find nothing more frustrating than students who insist on being told what it is they are to do so that they can parrot the information back. Unable or unwilling to undergo the work and risk that genuine learning requires, they stand ready to learn right answers that grade books can record.

3. *Subjective knowledge:* Here, truth and knowledge are conceived of as being personal, private, subjectively known or intuited. Often there is a turning away from external authority and a turning toward those people who share one's experience. Frequently, I see myself and my teaching partners who seek to work holistically in this category. Authority depends upon being one of the group, of doing the work, of sharing a common experience. People are quick to come together with their confederates, and teachers know this better than anyone. It is this knowledge that enables teachers to bring and keep learning communities together. As a teacher, I try to work alongside students of silence to help them gain a footing in this kind of knowing, to be a part of a group that values highly the personal knowledge and experiences of group members.

4. *Procedural knowledge:* Expert knowledge and objective procedures for obtaining and communicating knowledge are valued. Schooling exists to ensure that learning goes on better than it otherwise would. Therefore, knowledge that is arrived at in studied ways is of foremost importance. The challenge of teaching and learning here is the ability to critique knowledge and events and to grow in one's knowledge about the world.

5. *Constructed knowledge:* Knowledge in this category is viewed as contextual. People experience themselves as creators of knowledge and value both subjective and objective strategies for knowing. Knowing that is felt to be intuitively and personally important is integrated with knowledge that is learned from others, including authorities. Holistic teachers pitch their teaching toward helping students to see themselves as people who constitute meaning based on experience and content.

Teachers know the truth of these categories. The stories we hold most dear are those that tell of the silent student whose voice we helped to discover. We fuss at the beginning of the year with students who are content to wait to be told what to do, who perceive themselves as receivers of discoveries made by other people. We take delight when students begin to speak from the authority of their own experience and work to nudge them along a pathway that will demonstrate the value of critiquing knowledge constructed by others. The orientation of holistic teaching and learning is to bring students to value the constructed character of knowledge, to view knowledge as contextual, and to accept responsibility for entering into the process of interpretation and revision. Authority from a holistic perspective is not for controlling but for empowering students.

When viewed as a process and not as a thing, authority encompasses acts of imagination and interpretation, making it open to continued examination and revision. It is always possible to imagine an alternative to existing relationships where authority is involved. Just as long as someone is willing to look anew at what is happening, change is possible.

The question remains how to conceptualize authority in a way that is consistent with holistic and democratic values. Sennett (1980) suggests two very appropriate criteria that those in positions of authority might be expected to meet. The demands are that authority be visible and legible. "Visible means that those who are in positions of control be explicit about themselves: clear about what they can and cannot do; explicit about their promises. Legible specifies how this open statement could come about" (168).

In the learning community, these two demands can function as guidelines for helping students understand authority by positioning them to reflect on authority relationships. The situation might be one in which a person is exercising group leadership or is controlling or influencing another person.

I find the idea of teachers and students working together to make authority legible exciting. Together, in dialogue, community members can work at "reading" authority, understanding power relationships, and nurturing democratic attitudes. Sennett (1980) writes:

> All the ideas of democracy that we inherited from the 18th Century are based on the notion of visible, legible authority. The citizens are to read together; they are to observe the conditions of society and discuss them with one another. The result of this common effort is that the citizens entrust certain powers to the leaders, and judge the leaders on how well they merit that trust. The conditions of trust are to be entirely visible; the leader, Jefferson says, may use discretion, but may not be permitted to keep his intentions to himself. (168–69).

Excellent opportunities to study the makeup of authority are certain to arise on the playground, in the classroom, in the school offices, and in the community. There will be opportunities to examine authority that is nurturing and restrained, just as there will be occasions to study authority that is pursued arbitararily, without regard for the people involved. The most fruitful insights will come, of course, from experiences where students have immediate access to the facts and where the meaning is lived. Coming together in small and large groups to study the makeup of authority is certain to be a unique event in the lives of most students. Few will have had the opportunity to discuss with people in charge the intentions that guide them in their actions or would even think of doing so.

Consider the learning that occurs when a teacher joins with students to understand motivations and to uncover ways that people make use of power for reasons that both serve the welfare of the group and selfish interests. At the most basic level, teachers can work to make their intentions known. It is simply a matter of making sure than when in our teaching we make a truly important decision for an individual or the group, we call on others to ask us why we have made the decision. Once the reasons are given, we then give time for them to discuss have imput. We cannot empower students if we are not open and seek their assent. It is important not to neglect that as students interpret and imagine alternatives to what we have proposed, they have opportunities to experience themselves as meaning makers, not passive receivers of someone else's meaning.

A learning community that seeks to make authority visible and legible can surely strengthen democratic ideals. Democracies need people who are knowledgeable about the nature of authority and can imagine alternatives to what exists. The quality of life in a democratic society depends on people's ability to critique what *is* in the light of what *might be*. Democracy is served when people have no fear of authority but recognize it for what it is and are ready to work for change when and if needed.

12

Life Activities

*L*earning results from action and reflection. All of us—students, teachers, children, adults—learn when we take action and then reflect, that is reach judgments about what we have done. Taking a critical look at what we do is a priority where learning is concerned because it slows us down and raises the question of whether what *is* (the results of our acting) is what it should be. Through reflection, the possibility exists that we can exercise a degree of control over our lives. The teaching intent is to ensure that students pose problems and construct meaning, that they take action and intervene on their own behalf in learning encounters. On the students' part, teachers call for "wide-awakeness," in the sense that Maxine Greene (1973) uses the term, meaning that they give their full attention to life and their relatedness to the world. I will illustrate the point with an example related to writing.

Imagine that a teacher assigns students to write in journals daily but then gives no attention to the work other than allowing time for it. It's not likely that students will become more perceptive in attending to their lives, grow in writing fluency, or develop a sense of audience and voice. On the other hand, the teacher who takes an interest in the students' lives and make genuine responses to them gives students a reason to think about the value of their work, leading them to be aware of what they are doing in their writing as well as imaging how to do it better.

Holistic teachers try to create learning situations that are connected to life. This implies that the work itself, as well as how it is undertaken, is in agreement with the activities that are part of our daily living. The term "life activities" was a result of an interview with a group of fifth and sixth graders in Karen Smith's class who had developed an interesting interpretation of Chris Van Allsburg's book *The Stranger*. I asked them to share their thinking with me. The students pointed out that while the interpretation of the text they developed was interesting and fun, it was only part of what was important about their work. They explained that the way in which they had worked together in studying the book was how they would be expected to work in real life, once they were out of school and making a living. They had shared interpretations, negotiated meaning when questions arose, and together constructed an interpretation of the text they found satisfying—at least for the time being. As one boy said, "I'm sure someone will see it a different way tomorrow." Life activities are not reading to answer schoolbook questions at the end of a chapter or practicing to improve scores on an achievement test, but are what people do in real life. When we are involved with life activities we:

- Plan and complete joint projects

- Collaborate

- Negotiate meaning

- View our own and the work of others from a critical perspective

- Care for others

Life activities will succeed only to the extent that they include content that is compelling to students. Only then can students engage in the inquiry, critiquing, and mess of meaning making that are all part of daily living. There is no place for far-off goals—a characteristic of fragmented instruction that isolates learning skills now so that real work can be done correctly later on. Purpose and the immediacy of students' lives are valued. Writers communicate ideas to interested audiences. Joint projects are undertaken in science that require curiosity, initiative, and imagination. Readers study literature for the immediate enjoyment it will bring, as well as a way of knowing that challenges and enriches the imagination.

There are five criteria for life activities:

1. Involve students in the expression (construction) of meaning and in critiquing the results for the purpose of improved understanding.
2. Maintain the usefulness of language.
3. Seek to make learning encounters responsive to students' backgrounds, experiences, and intentions.
4. Recognize the social aspect of knowing by keeping the learning encounter open so that contributions can be made by others.
5. Support students in exercising authority and in taking responsibility for their own learning.

Now, I'd like to expand on the notion of life activities by examining other important traits.

Essence

The intrinsic nature of an activity can only be experienced by actively participating. Holistic teaching values attending to the essence of an activity, whether it's being a writer, a reader, a dancer, a mathematician, or a scientist. Therefore, teaching and learning is not a one, two, three drill: first do this and then that. Holistic teachers are concerned that students dwell in the meaning they are learning about. *There is no rush to develop meaning.* Students are encouraged to slow down, to pay attention, to discuss their progress with others and to keep in touch with their feeling and thinking as they work.

Experiencing in a nonreflective way that is more physical than intellectual is important. For example, from a holistic perspective, it's not enough that students have a textbook knowledge of how governments function. Beyond knowledge about the history and functions of government, there is the essence of political activity and governing. Consequently, a government for the learning community might be formed, a laboratory for students to experience taking decision-making powers into their own hands, being candidates for leadership, experiencing the process of persuading others, and accepting responsibility and exercising control.

Feeling is a way of knowing. There is a feeling side to hitting a baseball just as there is a feeling to participating in a political or literary discussion, to writing, to solving equations, and to dancing. Practiced teachers know that the attitude and behavior of learners involved in an activity can often tell us more about how they're progressing and the actual products they make.

I recently observed an eight-year-old student writing. Eyes to the ceiling, pencil clenched in teeth, she contemplated. Then in a flash, she made a decision and plunged ahead in her writing, only to stop in a short time to repeat the action. Her expression signaled that she knew more about what it was to write than what appeared on the paper. I asked her how she had decided on what to put down on the paper. Her response that "it felt right" is in keeping with what guides accomplished writers. All learners benefit from experiencing the essence of knowing, of doing, of being. The entire body is a way of knowing.

Knowing the essence of an activity pulls us forward when our rational powers are blocked. Holistic teachers teach essence, and when essence is perceived, they teach what's necessary to expand the perception. First they emphasize lived experiences, and then students are helped to develop their expression by reflecting upon it.

Openness

Holistic learning environments, constructed to support life activities, are characterized by openness. Openness means that experiences are kept open to reinterpretations. As long as there is a student or group willing to take up a point of view, original meaning can be expressed. Suspense and surprise are possible. Meaning fluctuates, open to critique and reinterpretation that is responsive to individual and group inquiry. Perceptions, however naive, are valued as fertile ground for original insights. Openness acknowledges the importance of the person in making meaning. Teachers value the fact that students want to hear a story again, realizing that the possibility exists for it yielding new insights. And they welcome students wanting to study a topic studied a previous year. Life possibilities are constantly emerging for those who can respond imaginatively to encounters.

Teachers are concerned about the student's purpose for undertaking work. Once a student has a project underway, problems will arise that must be confronted and worked through. In life activities there is work to do, but no fixed hierarchy of skills to be mastered. Students are not pushed along a prescribed route toward predetermined destinations. Quite the opposite. In life activities, students individually, in pairs, and in groups hike their way along varied terrain that is sometimes rocky and steep and without trail markers. In life activities, with the help of others, students make their own way, solving problems as they go and assuming responsibility for their own learning. Teachers, as experienced hikers, having been over the terrain before, study the hiker's ways. When difficulty is anticipated, teachers move alongside their students to watch how they work, appreciate their efforts, help reflect on where they have been and where they are headed, identify problems they are encountering, and set reasonable destinations. Possibilities are sketched out and choices are made.

Opportunities to learn arise in life activities as students contend with collecting, evaluating, organizing, and reporting information. It is within the process of making observations, interpreting texts, keeping records, conducting interviews, making surveys, studying artifacts, and developing ways of reporting results to others that chances for learning exist. When learning activities are authentic, teachers do not need to make up problems for students to solve. They are naturally present in the work.

Life activities are open to the interests, expectations, and initiatives that originate in both the learning community and the everyday community. And equally important, students take up activities in ways that are in keeping with how work is conducted beyond the classroom walls.

History

Life activities contribute to both a personal and a shared history. Each community member influences the evolution of the community and contributes to its history. Community history is influenced by all of the actions taken. To put it another way, history is not a commodity that can be purchased. It must be brought into existence by actively doing.

Early in the school year—before a sense of belonging and trust have evolved, before studies have been undertaken and projects completed, before students have learned to collaborate effectively and negotiate meaning, before there is trust—the results of even the very best efforts of making and doing are a bit skimpy. Nonetheless, they are important for the future. Each encounter leaves behind a residue of meaning that contributes to the shared history, thereby enriching the meaning-making potential of the group. That is why teachers save favorite books for literature study until mid-year when the group's history has evolved sufficiently to support the rigors of a challenging dialogue. The importance of history to learning is another argument for having a teacher stick with a group for more than one year or for having multi-age groupings so that each year there are community members who are familiar with one another's ways. That way, there is a fertile seed bed for genuine learning early in the year.

As months pass, the potential for learning develops both diversity and depth. And as it does, its potential for supporting learning increases. Classmates' knowing one another's ways, interests, and strengths builds confidence in one another, thereby contributing greatly to collaborative efforts. All of this comes about through working together. Conferencing that results in a good story being written, caring that strengthens students' self-esteem, participation in a rigorous and joyful celebration, and facing up to problems and collaborating to solve them all add to the shared history. Personal relationships are as important as interest and purpose in conducting a study that requires student imagination and initiative. A good study in social studies or literature can greatly enrich the field-of-meaning and with it the potential for future action. It does so by generating knowledge about the world that was absent before the study, plus alternative ways of viewing and interpreting what is happening in the world.

A classroom community, like any other community, needs people who can interpret group history in light of the present. It is the way of human beings to make connections with our past and use them to envision the future. People gather around newborns and talk about how they look like members of their families. Candidates for office can expect to have their life history examined for clues that indicate their character and suggest how they will respond to problems.

In holistic learning communities, continuity is constructed in the light of individuals' lives and the shared life of the social body. Holistically oriented teaching and learning stand apart from traditional education in which an attempt is made to control continuity by means of prescribed curricula, textbooks, and the like. Coherence—students' awareness of their continuity with the past and their ability to see possibilities—is an important characteristic of holistic learning communities. Admittedly, the past is not made up of personal relationships alone. It is based on knowing about selections of the world's meaning as well. This is yet another reason that teachers with a holistic orientation favor multi-age groups and sticking with the same students for two or three years.

For a learning community to be truly effective, the group needs to work from a rich knowledge base. This base takes effort and learning and time to come into existence. If we want students to work in critical and complicated ways, they have to work with knowledge that will sustain such activity. The learning communities made by Kittye Copeland and her students are the richest intellectually and socially that I know of. Not only is Kittye a superb teacher, it helps that students are with her for five or six years. The knowledge base the community draws upon is exceedingly diverse and complex. The complexity of the judicial, governmental, and economic system that are central to the learning community are richer than anything I could imagine being made. Subject matter is not presented as facts to be learned. It is organized into disciplines that provide students with flexible perspectives for understanding what is happening in their world and gaining insight into solving problems. Young students are initiated into this complicated community life through lived experiences, and in time contribute to its development.

Teachers are the chief historians in the learning community. They interpret, enliven, and enrich the present by putting it in the context of the group's shared history. Linking the present with the past makes it possible to dignify effort and struggle, initiative and achievement, and growth. Meaningful lives do not just happen. The history of the past is constantly reinterpreted to draw into the light the significance of the present. As the year progresses, students increasingly play a part in interpreting the significance of what is happening. History is also a vehicle through which values can be clarified and dwelled upon without moralizing. It is an important way to care for the individual and collective welfare of the community.

The traits just discussed help to ensure that learning experiences will be genuine. In most schools, the actuality of experience is not a priority. Fake experiences produced by commercial publishers control the day. Students' desks, not just in the middle school but in first grade (over a dozen textbooks and workbooks in one school's first grade), are chucked full of textbooks and workbooks. (Storing them in an orderly way is a problem all in itself.) Students' lives are put on the shelf as they work their way through page after page and from book to book. Think, too, of checking the work, plus all the recordkeeping for a class of twenty-eight children. Give a moment of thought to the motivational problems involved in getting students to work their way through hundreds of hours of fake experiences.

Life in the holistic learning community is directed toward authentic experience. Lived experiences are what is valued because they nurture language and conceptual development. This means that the division of experience into subject matter categories becomes blurred. The most important concern is the quality of the experience, genuinely engaging students in feeling and intellect, aesthetically and emotionally, not a particular topic of study.

From a holistic perspective, teaching–learning begins with the student, not a teacher's manual. To do their work, the teacher and students need access to a wealth of materials, not stodgy textbooks that are bland, if not boring, and frequently out-of-date. The world is a dynamic place, and students have a right to be alive to what is evolving. In their daily living, students are immersed in information; it makes sense to create orderly places where they can work at making sense of what is happening in their lives and the world. Holistically oriented teaching seeks to come to grips with the actuality of experience.

Disciplines and subject matter areas are no more than vehicles of differing sorts—ways of viewing that are open to revision—that are useful for illuminating experience, for providing an angle of vision, for individual sense making (Greene 1973). But, their function is to *extend* experience, not serve as a *substitute* for experience. And they are open to revision when discoveries are made and they are found to be inadequate for responding to problems.

One's entire body can be thought of as a way of knowing from a holistic perspective. We depend in our living on tacit knowing, meaning that exists beyond words and cannot be spelled out in so many words. In the absence of linguistic clues, we see things, hear things, feel things, move about, explore our surroundings, and get to know his or her way about (Polyanyi 1958). We have all participated in rituals and celebrations, as well as given ourselves in play at a level that is best understood as *undergoing* experience. People can understand without being able to openly express the joy and sorrow they experience in listening to a violinist give a superb concert, the awe felt when a center fielder runs down a ball that at first seemed clearly beyond reach. The significance of particular pieces of music and books in our lives, or the joy of being with friends can, like the experience of love, exist beyond words, since words fall short of revealing what is truly experienced.

Conclusion

Why is holism important in education? Because our schools are, after all, made up of people, and people are complex and many-sided. People are not merely "I think" beings. We encounter the world and express our experience in numerous and varied ways. Greene (1973) suggests that "the ability to know is only one feature of the self, that the self must not be identified with reason or with mind. To speak of the self is to speak of an individual's body as well as his mind, his past as well as his present; the world in which he is involved, the others with whom he is continually engaged" (136).

Holistic teaching is an alternative to teaching that makes a "mind" project of students, fragmenting learning and separating the head and the heart. It is an alternative to studying content chopped into basic skills and assembled for delivery to passive minds. Traditional educational talk is about skills, sub-skills, and skill mastery, never heart, trust, faith, belief, and feeling. Students are uprooted from their lived experiences, marched through skill sequences, whatever the content, and judged for mastery and remediated as prescribed. The intent is to educate the intellect, which is treated as if it existed independent of a living person. Tests are given and remedial classes are organized purely on the basis of performance on tests designed to meet predetermined objectives. Students are then skilled and drilled again without involving them in actually doing, making something. The results of these efforts are as predictable as the Friday spelling tests. Kids might score high on Friday, but the chances are good that what they have "learned" will not carry over to their real life writing. In contrast, holism believes that it is the way of people to work at making sense of their experience and that each person is the center of his or her knowing. Inasmuch as holism asserts that feeling is a way of knowing, what happens cannot always be explained in the language that has traditionally governed educational discourse. Traditional bureaucratic ways of organizing for education have given authority over what happens in the classroom to outsiders. Holistic education requires people who are going to have the say to be insiders, those who know the pulse of community life, those who truly know what is going on.

If problems in learning were merely a matter of the intellect, the educational technologies marketed to ensure learning would have succeeded and education would not be floundering. It is unfortunate that educators and politicians responded to the lack of learning by increasing the emphasis on skill instruction, increased fragmentation, and preaching accountability. That is, higher-ups in the chain of command decide what it is teachers and students will do and teachers are held accountable. Teachers on the one hand are asked to be submissive to authority and on the other to provide "excellence" to the students they teach. Educational opportunities that students deserve depend on teachers' overthrowing the role they are charged with—that of being a technician. It is up to us to think for ourselves and to refuse to act out someone else's plan. Strength will come from understanding the thinking that guides our practice and by giving voice to our varied visions of what might be. After all, who's in those classrooms everyday? Who else is in a position to have the experience, the insight, and the imagination required to bring about reform?

Holism considers it an error to teach solely to the intellect. Intellect and feeling, mind and body, are connected. Each aspect of self is part of all other aspects. A human being and social situations are not without life, mere objects to be manipulated and judged from a distance. All people are dependent upon tacit knowing, emotional knowing, intuitive knowing, body knowing, and not merely rational knowing. Teaching that is intended to enhance the intellect is strengthened by recognizing this, not weakened. We are social in every aspect of our existence. The place, the learning community, is of greatest importance for it is within the group that we come to value who we are and what we can do. Students in residence, confident in themselves and trusting of others, are in a position to take charge of their learning.

In education, there have always been metaphors that present an image of education leading to the child's unfolding and awakening. But with the exception of individual teachers and a few schools, the image has never managed more than a foothold in educational practice. Now that education is in a crisis, perhaps the time is right for hearing the voices of teachers who know how to respond to the whole child to be heard. Katherine Paterson, in *The Spying Heart* (1989), uses a metaphor I find inspiring. Paterson contemplates the split between heart and mind. She writes, "Among the many Chinese and Japanese ideographs for our word *idea* is one that combines the character for *sound* with the character for *heart*— the heart being the seat of the intelligence as well as of emotion. Thus, an idea is something that makes a sound in the heart" (45).

There is no question that life in classrooms is crowded. And making learning communities—coming together, keeping together, and learning together—is not easy. It is far easier to dominate and require obedience. But if the prospect of encouraging the social nature of learning lets our students experience genuine learning and helps them to uncover ideas that make a sound in their hearts, isn't that a compelling argument for trying?

Bibliography

Baylor, B. 1986. *I'm in Charge of Celebrations.* New York: Scribner's.

Berger, P., and Luckmann, T. 1967. *The Social Construction of Reality.* Garden City, New York: Doubleday and Company, Inc.

Belenky, M., Clinchy, B., Goldberger, N., and Tarule, J. 1986. *Women's Ways of Knowing.* New York: Basic Books.

Buber, M. 1969. *Men of Dialogue.* New York: Funk & Wagnalls.

Cox, H. 1969. *The Feast of Fools.* New York: Harper & Row.

Dewey, J. 1930. *Construction and Criticism.* New York: Columbia University Press.

Edelsky, E., Altwerger, B., and Flores, B. 1991. *Whole Language: What's the Difference.* Portsmouth, N.H.: Heinemann.

Estes, E. 1972. *The Hundred Dresses.* New York: Harcourt Brace Jovanovich.

Forbes, E. 1943. *Johnny Tremain.* Boston: Houghton Mifflin.

Freire, P. 1970. *Pedagogy of the Oppressed.* New York: Herder & Herder.

Gennep, A. 1960. *The Rites of Passage.* Chicago: University of Chicago Press.

Greene, M. 1973. *Teacher as Stranger.* Belmont, Calif.: Wadsworth.

Gusdorff, G. 1965. *Speaking.* Evanston, Ill.: Northwestern University Press.

Hamilton, V. 1974. *M.C. Higgins the Great.* New York: Macmillan.

Kwant, R. 1967. *Critique: Its Nature and Function.* Pittsburgh: Duquesne University Press.

Kwant, R. 1965. *Phenomenology of Language.* Pittsburgh: Duquesne University Press.

Kwant, R. 1965. *The Phenomenology of Social Existence.* Pittsburgh: Duquesne Unuversity Press.

Langer, S. 1951. *Philosophy in a New Key.* New York: The New American Library.

Luijpen, W. 1969. *Existential Phenomenology.* Pittsburgh: Duquesne University Press.

Mayeroff, M. 1971. *On Caring.* New York: Harper & Row.

Oakeshott, M. 1959. *The Voice of Poetry in the Conservation of Mankind.* London: Bowes & Bowes.

Ogden, J. 1897. *The Art of Teaching.* Cincinnati: The Eclectic Press.

Polyanyi, M. 1964. *Personal Knowledge.* New York: Harper & Row.

Sewell, E. 1964. *The Human Metaphor.* Notre Dame, Ind.: University of Notre Dame Press

Sennett, R. 1980. *Authority.* London: Secker & Warburg.

Vygotsky, I.S. 1978. *Mind in Society.* Ed. M. Cole, V. John-Steiner, S. Scribner, and E. Souberman. Cambridge, Mass.: Harvard University Press.

Waller, W. 1965. *The Sociology of Teaching.* New York: John Wiley & Sons.

Wells, G. 1986. *The Meaning Makers.* Portsmouth, N.H.: Heinemann.

Wilde, O. 1978. *The Selfish Giant.* New York: Methuen.

Yashima, T. 1955. *Crow Boy.* New York: Viking Press.